Advertising

Information or Manipulation?

Nancy Day

Enslow Publishers, Inc.

44 Fadem Road   PO Box 38
Box 699   Aldershot
Springfield, NJ 07081   Hants GU12 6BP
USA   UK

http://www.enslow.com

Library of Congress Cataloging-in-Publication Data

Day, Nancy.
    Advertising: information or manipulation? / Nancy Day.
       p. cm. — (Issues in focus)
    Includes bibliographical references and index.
    Summary: Discusses how advertising has developed, how
companies use it to entice consumers, and the impact of
advertising on people, particularly young people.
    ISBN 0-7660-1106-2
    1. Advertising—Juvenile literature. 2. Advertising—Psychological
aspects—Juvenile literature. 3. Persuasion (Psychology)—Juvenile literature.
[1. Advertising.] I. Title. II. Series: Issues in focus (Springfield, NJ)
HF5829.D39 1999
659.1'01'9—dc21   98-35032
                                          CIP
                                          AC

Printed in the United States of America

10 9 8 7 6 5 4 3 2 1

To Our Readers:
All internet addresses in this book were active and appropriate when
we went to press. Any comments or suggestions can be sent by e-mail to
Comments@enslow.com or to the address on the back cover.

Illustration Credits: Illustration Credits: Bozell Worldwide, Inc.
Advertising, 26; California Department of Health Services, 83;
Hershey Foods Corporation, 94; Levi Strauss & Co., 60, 67, 72;
Courtesy of the Library of Congress, 33, 44, 54, 63, 88; The
McGraw-Hill Companies, 9; Nike Corporation, 91; The Pillsbury
Corporation, 22; Xerox Corporation, 19.

Cover Illustration: New York Convention & Visitors Bureau.

Contents

In our factory, we make lipstick;
in our advertising, we sell hope.

—Charles Revson, founder of Revlon Cosmetics

1

Creating Want

Definition of Advertising: "It makes you spend money you don't have for something you don't want."

—Will Rogers

Congratulations! It's a baby boy. As he leaves the hospital, his parents are given coupons for Pampers diapers, samples of Johnson & Johnson baby soap, and free cans of Enfamil liquid formula. Within days, his family will be deluged with mailings and phone calls offering everything from free portraits to a savings plan for college. Before he is two, he will be able to recognize some brand names and maybe even sing a few advertising jingles. By age

5

three, he'll have to have the character doll from his favorite television show and the McDonald's cup promoting the latest Disney movie. By seven, he'll demand the newest release in the latest collectible fad, and he will be receiving about twenty thousand advertising messages a year on television alone. By nine, he'll want the shoes his favorite basketball player wears, and he'll be able to recite beer commercials. At thirteen, he won't be caught dead wearing the wrong brand of jeans, and he will have his own entry in the huge data banks that marketing firms keep on consumers.[1]

Why Is There So Much Advertising?

The sheer volume of advertising is staggering. Studies estimate that each American sees sixteen thousand advertisements (including logos, labels, and announcements) in a single day.[2] The average house receives thirty-four pounds of advertising messages by mail each year, for a total of 4.5 million tons of junk mail in America's mailboxes annually.[3] United States companies spent $187.5 billion on advertising in 1997, and experts expected annual spending to rise to nearly $200 billion in 1998.[4]

Every day, Americans are bombarded with advertising messages. The medium might be a television or radio ad, an outdoor billboard, a newspaper or magazine ad, a movie that shows a star using a particular product, or a catalog or flyer mailed to homes. Or the medium might be a message sent over the Internet, a company-sponsored school program, a promotional e-mail, a sporting event or concert "brought to you by" a particular company, a logo printed on a T-shirt, a blimp flying overhead, or an imprinted pencil from a dentist. The packages products come in are also a form of advertising. If you don't believe it, picture the cereal aisle at the supermarket displaying rows of grain-filled plastic bags instead of colorful boxes displaying offers of free prizes and contests.

Consumer advertising (advertising directed to the general public) is just one form of advertising. Companies also advertise to each other. Raw material producers promote their products to the companies that use them in manufacturing. These companies may then advertise to companies that buy products in bulk or wholesale. Wholesalers advertise to retailers, and retailers then advertise to consumers. Drug companies advertise to doctors, publishers advertise to librarians, locker manufacturers advertise to schools, and computer companies advertise to everybody. Institutions and organizations promote their interests. Political candidates advertise to voters. The government advertises the postal service, military recruitment, and so on. Even advertising agencies advertise to the companies they hope will use their services to create . . . more advertising.

What Does Advertising Do?

Advertising informs. Suppose you invent a new product. No matter how good it is, you won't sell many of them unless you are able to tell people that the product exists, explain how it is better than other products (bigger, cheaper, faster, more effective), and let them know where to buy it. That is what advertising does. If the entire concept of your product is new, you may even need to tell potential buyers why they need it. If others create products just like yours, you will *really* need advertising to convince people to buy your product instead.

Advertising persuades. By playing on emotions and appealing to the need to belong, it transforms a cancer-causing device (cigarettes) into a ticket to popularity and success. It takes a combination of chemicals and oils (perfume) and promises romance. It demonstrates how you can be smarter, prettier, thinner, and more successful; how you can smell better, get rich quicker, and make friends more easily; how you can avoid embarrassment, meet a mate, build a happy family, and have really great breath. It convinces you that you want solutions to problems you didn't know existed and desire products to meet needs you didn't even know you had. It shows you as you wish you were. It sells dreams.

Advertising tells you what you need. Before advertisers told us to, who worried about dandruff? Who was embarrassed by teeth that weren't blinding white, toilets that didn't smell fresh, or water spots on drinking glasses? Who knew that houses had to be deodorized with perfume-packed sprays, plug-in devices, stick-on scent dispensers, potpourri, simmering herbs, and odor neutralizers?

Advertising isn't all bad, however. By paying for advertising space, companies fund most of what you read in magazines and books, what you hear on the radio, and what you watch on television. It also increasingly pays for what is on the Internet.

Advertising also educates. It informs us about candidates running for office. It tells us about important issues such as the benefits of seatbelt use, the dangers of drugs, and the problem of drunk driving.

" I don't know who you are.

I don't know your company.

I don't know your company's product.

I don't know what your company stands for.

I don't know your company's customers.

I don't know your company's record.

I don't know your company's reputation.

Now – what was it you wanted to sell me?"

Sales start **before** you call—with business-to-business advertising.

The McGraw·Hill Companies

Financial Services. Information and Media. Educational and Professional Publishing.

Advertising performs an important role in informing the public about products and services.

It explains how to use products, gives us recipes, and demonstrates ways in which we can change our homes and places of business. It teaches us grooming habits. Unfortunately, it can also teach us that to be accepted one must speak English without an accent and be thin, rich, good-looking, successful, and white. It can reinforce racial, cultural, and sexual stereotypes. It can make us unsatisfied with who we are, greedy for what we don't have, and oblivious to the miseries of millions who haven't a fraction of the comforts we take for granted.

Advertising Through the Years

Advertising is not new. In ancient Greece, merchants in the marketplaces called out promotional messages to potential customers, people put up posters offering rewards for escaped slaves, and cities provided jugs of olive oil to be given as prizes for athletic games as a way to promote their cities' products. Buying, selling, and trading are ancient concepts, and along with them comes the need to tell others what you have and why they should want it.

The development of advertising as a sophisticated marketing tool is much more recent. As the Industrial Revolution ended and products were produced in mass quantities, companies began needing to sell products in large numbers.

Advertising agencies, the companies that create and place advertising, emerged in the mid-1800s. Initially, agents were hired by newspaper publishers to make contact with potential advertisers. The agents received a percentage, or *commission*, on the sale of ad space. Agents began acting as middlemen, taking orders for space from advertisers and then buying the space from the newspapers. Later, they bought quantities of space in advance and then resold it to numerous advertisers, keeping the commissions from the publications. (Even today, advertising agencies receive their commissions from the publishers, not the clients.) It wasn't until the late 1800s that advertising agencies first started to create ads for their clients' products.[5]

In the early days of advertising, publishers lied about the number of subscribers their newspapers had and advertising agents lied about whether ads had appeared. Advertisers also lied about their products. And companies began to see the power of advertising: It enabled them to sell almost anything to almost anyone. "I can advertise *dish water*, and sell it, just as well as an article of merit," bragged a patent-medicine marketer. "It is all in the advertising."[6]

Until the late 1800s there were only three forms of advertising: handbills and circulars (small printed pieces to be distributed), outdoor signs, and newspapers. Then a new medium, magazines, was created.

Advertisers quickly saw the potential to reach people through this new form of entertainment. Some magazines carried no advertising (except from their own publishers), others accepted only a few ads, but gradually advertising became a major portion of many magazines. As early as 1909 humorist Finley Peter Dunne had his fictional creation Mr. Dooley ironically complaining that he had bought his favorite magazine only to find that over a fourth of it was literature. He had started to read an ad and soon discovered it was really an article! "A man don't want to dodge around through almost impenethrable pomes an' reform articles to find a pair iv suspinders or a shavin' soap," he griped.[7]

Advertising fees allowed the publishers to charge consumers less for the magazines and helped fund the *editorial* content (the articles and other content supplied by the magazine). "Do you know why we publish the *Ladies' Home Journal*?" Cyrus Hermann Kotzschmar Curtis, the magazine's publisher, asked advertisers in the late 1800s. "The editor thinks it is for the benefit of American women. That is an illusion. . . . The real reason . . . is to give you people who manufacture things that American women want and buy a chance to tell them about your products."[8]

Critics began to emerge as advertising became a larger and more visible part of American life. "Advertising is being read more and more, and I am sorry to say that some of it does not have a good moral effect," said social crusader Jane Addams in 1913.[9]

During the 1920s advertisers, fearing their ads were getting lost in the increasing commercial din, began to try new tactics. Some companies tried to scare people into buying their products. "A single contact with inferior toilet tissue," warned Scott Paper Company in 1928, "may start the way for serious infection—and a long and painful illness."[10] Listerine featured a cautionary tale (titled "Her Last Party") of a woman who ventured home from a party without taking the precaution of gargling with Listerine. She caught a chill—and died.[11]

More than anything else, advertisers during the 1920s tried to make consumers dissatisfied with the things they had in order to fuel new purchases. Companies developed ads that stressed the need to buy new and better products. They worked to convince consumers that they could buy happiness by making the right product choices. By creating this preoccupation with possessing products, advertisers helped build the modern consumption-based lifestyle.

Although it initially had no commercials, radio, like magazines, grew with the financial help of advertising. Radio advertising was a challenge: There could be no visuals, only sound. But radio had the advantage of intruding into people's homes and reaching the one adult in twenty who couldn't read. In addition, listeners couldn't simply turn the page; they were a captive audience. For this reason, advertisers were initially concerned that radio ads would create ill will. In 1925 *Printer's Ink*, an advertising trade magazine, cautioned that "the family circle is not a public place, and advertising has no business intruding there unless it is invited."[12] But advertisers soon found the tremendous power of mass media: to reach many regions of the country and appeal to different classes of people, all with a single message.

Advertising Becomes Inescapable

Television revolutionized advertising. From the beginning, television was celebrated as "the vacuum cleaner salesman's dream."[13] Hazel Bishop lipstick sales grew from $50,000 to $4.5 million in two years from television advertising alone.[14] Between 1945 and 1950 advertising expenditures grew from $2.9 billion to $5.7 billion.[15]

Advertisers produced and sponsored entire programs such as *Kraft Television Theater, Goodyear TV Playhouse*, and *Texaco Star Theater*. Sponsorship provided a wide range of good programs, but the line between advertising and programming began to blur, with stars pitching products and entertainment blending with promotion. "Today, the sponsors pull the strings and we are the puppets," complained comedian Groucho Marx in 1953. "Radio and television announcers have to be liars."[16] The television networks worried about the amount of control advertisers were able to exercise through sponsorships but needed the money to fund this new and expensive medium.

In the early 1950s, the idea of spot advertising began to develop. Smaller advertisers who couldn't afford a full sponsorship could pay for fifteen minutes of programming. Networks would have four sponsors for a one-hour show rather than one (and they could charge higher rates per minute for the shorter time blocks).

Suddenly, the content of television changed. The networks began to develop programs designed to attract the most advertisers: programs that would reach the greatest number of people and put them in the right mood for buying. Live performances of works by contemporary authors and productions of great literary dramas gave way to safe mainstream programming that wouldn't have people mulling over plot complexities when the toothpaste ads came on.

The ads changed as well. Advertisers began to create loud, aggressive, repetitive ads that would stand out from the growing number of competing messages.

The Hidden Persuaders

As advertising began to enter American homes and minds with greater frequency, criticism grew. Some people questioned whether advertising might be worse than just irritating. Could it actually be dangerous?

In 1957, *The Hidden Persuaders* by Vance Packard became a best-seller. Packard argued that advertisers were consciously attempting "to channel our unthinking habits, our purchasing decisions, and our thought processes by the use of insights gleaned from psychiatry and the social sciences."[17] Packard warned that *motivational research*, a technique advertisers were using to determine what was going on in consumers' minds in order to create effective ads, had the potential to become mind control.

Consumer fears grew even more after word spread that a movie theater had used *subliminal advertising*, hidden messages that could make people want things without their being aware that they had seen any advertising. James M. Vicary, in an effort to promote his Subliminal Projection Company, announced that messages urging audience members to buy popcorn and soda, flashed on the screen so briefly that people didn't consciously see them, had resulted in dramatic increases in viewers' purchases of those items. Although he refused to identify the theater or to provide any proof of his claim, the idea of being manipulated subconsciously raised a storm of protest.

In January 1958 the Federal Communications Commission (FCC) ordered a test of subliminal advertising. Vicary hid the message *eat popcorn* in a film shown to members of Congress and other dignitaries. It had no effect.[18] Nevertheless, the National Association of Broadcasters banned such messages from the airwaves.

Concerns over subliminal messages surfaced again in the 1970s when journalist Wilson Bryan Key suggested that sexual images and words were being secretly imbedded in advertisements in an attempt to manipulate consumers. He claimed to see the word *sex* in Ritz crackers advertisements, for example.[19] Although experts have now dismissed subliminal advertising as a hoax, the controversy strengthened consumers' distrust of advertising.

2

The Hows and Whys of Advertising

How Advertising Works

To get consumers to buy one product over another, advertisers create a *perceived difference* (a feeling in the consumer's mind that a particular product is different).

Sometimes the difference is simply the audience the company wants to target. Pepsi, for example, decided to promote its product as the soft drink for younger people ("the Pepsi Generation"). It created a young, hip image that appealed to status-conscious teenagers.

Advertisers target particular markets through *product positioning*. In the same way that you might groom, dress, and

17

present yourself in a way that telegraphs the kind of person you are, advertising "positions" a product so that people can sum up the product in an instant. Nick Shore, a partner in an agency that creates product *brands*, explains: "For example, you can look at a person, see chinos, a baseball cap turned backward, T-shirt, and think, 'O.K., I got it.'"[1] An image tells others what they can expect.

A brand of coffee might be positioned as a coffee for young urban singles (even though it may taste the same as a coffee being promoted to suburban house-wives). Ads would feature people who look the way young urban singles would like to see themselves: hip, successful, and witty. The ads would be placed in spots where the target audience would see them: urban newspapers, television programs popular with urban singles, subway stations, and trendy magazines. The coffee brand suddenly seems the cool choice for urban singles.

The Power of the Brand

The goal of most advertising is to create or maintain consumer loyalty to a particular brand of product. Advertisers do this by attaching some special value to the brand. The additional value may be something measurable like quality or special features, but more likely it will be something unmeasurable like glamour, hipness, or sex appeal.

Advertisers rely on the fact that people (particularly teenagers) are highly concerned with other people's opinions of them. They use the brand

When you use "Xerox" the way you use "aspirin," we get a headache.

X Boy, what a headache! And all because some of you may be using our name in a generic manner. Which could cause it to lose its trademark status the way the name "aspirin" did years ago. So when you do use our name, please use it as an adjective to identify our products and services, e.g., Xerox copiers. Never as a verb: "to Xerox" in place of "to copy", or as a noun: "Xeroxes" in place of "copies". Thank you. Now, could you excuse us, we've got to lie down for a few minutes.

THE
DOCUMENT
COMPANY
XEROX
Worldwide Sponsor

Companies do everything they can to protect valuable brand names.

to give the product an image that will impress people. By choosing the right brand, consumers are told, they will be viewed in a positive way by others.

Products sold through image advertising are promoted not for what they are but for the lifestyle they promise. The ads may never even show the product, but they convey an excitement, an image, a fantasy that consumers want.

Image-linked products can demand a high price, even though what the consumer gets is minimal. A small bottle of chemicals and oils may demand thirty dollars when sold as "maximum moisturizing skin toner" at the cosmetics counter. How does a company convince someone to pay that much? By promising love, success, power, acceptance—things much more valuable than the product itself.

Brand names and images can be worth a fortune. Imagine you could use the Nike "swoosh" for a day. You could put it on almost anything and be able to sell it! (Nike's "swoosh" is worth over $26 million a day, based on 1998 sales of $9.6 billion!)[2] That is why companies go to great lengths to protect their brands.

Brand names can be bought, sold, or even rented (licensed). When Ronson, a company known for its shavers and cigarette lighters, went out of business, the Ronson name was licensed to other companies to enhance their "unknown" products. Consumers, comfortable with the familiar name, bought these products without knowing that the Ronson company had nothing to do with them.[3]

Some companies gain brand visibility by creating a trademark character like the Jolly Green Giant or the Pillsbury Dough Boy. Characters attract attention, build recognition for a product, establish an image, and help consumers tell one brand from another. Now, characters are endorsing each other's products: Mr. Clean promotes Honda cars and Mr. Potato Head is "spokes-fry" for Burger King.[4]

Sometimes characters help position the product. In 1954 a cigarette manufacturer was searching for a way to portray its filter cigarette (which appealed mainly to women) as something men could smoke with pride. The managers asked themselves, "What is the most masculine type of man?" They came up with a cowboy, and the Marlboro Man was born.[5]

Celebrities have become brands, too. Michael Jordan, Martha Stewart, Tommy Hilfiger, and others have built empires selling diverse products that have only one thing in common: They have a celebrity name printed on them. When people buy these products, they are not buying the power of the perfume, the cut of the clothing, or the look of the linens so much as they are buying the image of the celebrity.

At least one noncelebrity has decided to create his own brand. Jesse Daggett, seventeen, read an article in *Fast Company* magazine by Tom Peters, a business adviser who described how anyone could make himself or herself into a brand-name product. Daggett, a clerk at a Dairy Queen, saw no reason why he couldn't create his own brand. "I like to think of the brand Jesse this way," he said. "Hard worker. Putting yourself in charge. If something needs to be done, Jesse can do it and get it done and be the leader of the team. That's the Jesse brand."[6]

Knowing Your Audience

The more advertisers know about their target audience, the more effective their advertising may be in convincing consumers to buy their product. Knowing what potential buyers desire, fear, and envy; what motivates them, how they think, and when they will act enables advertisers to tailor messages for maximum effectiveness. That is why companies spend

Invented characters increase a product's appeal and help consumers remember a brand.

millions of dollars on *marketing research.*

There are many kinds of marketing research. Companies may survey current or past customers. Or they may hire researchers to question shoppers at a mall. A more sophisticated version of this is the *focus group.*

A focus group is made up of people selected to represent the target audience for a product (for example, women eighteen to thirty-five with small children or doctors who write twenty or more prescriptions for antibiotics per day). The group meets in a room, usually equipped with a one-way mirror and recording equipment, where a facilitator guides them through a discussion about a product, an advertisement, or a brand name. For example, a company introducing a new cola for the youth market might show a group of teenagers a potential television ad. The facilitator would then ask, What might a person who buys the new brand look like? or Where might such a product be sold?

Most major companies routinely conduct marketing research. Money spent on research in the United States alone totaled over $4 billion in 1997.[7] Coca-Cola Company, for example, reportedly interviews at least one thousand people every three months from almost every country where Coke is sold.[8]

Some companies go even further to determine the consumer's "true" feelings. A company named House Calls sets up cameras in people's homes (with the participants' permission) to record the ways in which they interact with products. Honda and Toyota have actually arranged for staff members to live with families to observe how they use their cars. An advertising executive working on the Pioneer Stereo account rode around with the kind of men he hoped to sell car stereos to and later used phrases he had heard (such as "my drag racer of doom") in the advertising.[9]

Why Advertising Works

Advertisers use certain words and phrases they know will get attention and motivate people to buy. No matter how unremarkable the product, a good *copywriter* (someone who writes ads) can make it sound irresistible. Take the following ad:

"Miracle Product Solves Thousands of Problems"

Get the incredible product that has been used successfully by doctors, celebrities, sports superstars, and heads of state the world over! Made from the same organic material that is used in the manufacture of modern jetliners, it tackles an amazing number of challenges and can easily be recycled, helping preserve our precious

Have you seen me sweat? I must lose 10 lbs a game. And from what I hear, it's not just about losing water. It's about nutrients. That's why I drink milk. 2%. It's got nine essential nutrients my body needs, like calcium and potassium. I thought about telling the boys in Chicago, but it's about time they lost something.

The National Fluid Milk Processor Promotion Board uses the familiar "milk mustache" on famous people as a humorous way to promote the drinking of milk.

environment. This product's astonishing versatility is virtually unmatched. Its fast, its easy, and best of all, its inexpensive! Find out what millions of people already know. Order today.

Makes you want to run right out and buy one, doesn't it? Chances are, however, that you already have several. The miracle product is a rubber band.

The writer gets you going with attention-grabbers such as *miracle, astonishing, easy,* and *inexpensive.* Qualifiers (words that limit others) such as *virtually* and *helping* hardly register when used in such an environment. Words such as *organic* are only vaguely understood but sound good and lend credibility to the claim that the product is helping to protect the environment. Connections with high-technology products (such as a jetliner) and endorsements convince buyers, even if such boasts are (at least in the case of a rubber band) a bit of a stretch.

Phrases such as "find out what millions of people already know" are used to make consumers feel that they are really missing the boat if they don't buy the product because apparently everyone else is. Your judgment couldn't possibly be better than all those others' could it?

Advertisers make their ads stand out by using humor, ongoing story lines, unexpected dialogue, unusual techniques, attention-getting spokespersons, or simply by repeating the ads so often that people can't help but remember them. Faced with a choice between something familiar and the ominous "Brand X," most people choose the product they recognize.

Another way that advertisers get the attention of their audiences is through an authoritative presence. From the late 1950s through the 1960s, characters such as Mr. Clean, the Man from Glad, and the Ajax White Knight dropped in to reprimand women whose housekeeping skills weren't up to snuff. These days it's more often a disembodied voice that directs consumers, a technique called the *voice-over.*

In advertising to children and teens, marketers use models slightly older than their intended audience.[10] An older model fills the role of an authority figure by telling kids what is cool and what isn't. Kids tend to pay attention to (and imitate) what older kids say and do.

Advertising is a shorthand language. Its entire message must be communicated in thirty seconds, one page, or in the case of a billboard, a few words. One way to convey meaning is to use *stereotypes:* the confused old person, the rigid Japanese businessman, the swaggering African-American teen, the intimidating southern sheriff. Advertisers have neither the time nor the desire to present the complexities of real life. So they portray women who worry about which deodorant to use, men whose jobs hinge on whether their bosses approve of the overnight delivery service they choose, and teenagers who obsess about everything.

Stereotypes may seem amusing, but they can have a permanent impact. When we see members of a specific group of people repeatedly presented in a particular way, we begin to believe that all people of that group are the same way. Such impressions are hard to overcome. "Advertising is a very important form of education," says feminist Gloria Steinem, "It is estimated that 40 percent of all of our subcultural intake comes from advertising."[11]

Advertising More Than Products

Some advertising is designed to promote a company rather than a product. Corporate ads may be created to gain consumer acceptance, overcome an image problem, or promote the company name as a brand.

In the late 1980s the Du Pont company ran an ad that featured a man who had "lost both legs to a Vietcong rocket" playing basketball with the help of artificial limbs. While viewers were captivated by the visuals, the company explained that "researchers discovered that a Du Pont plastic could help make truly lifelike artificial limbs." Such an emotionally powerful ad helps consumers forget that Du Pont once made tritium and plutonium for nuclear weapons[12] and was called a "merchant of death" for profiting from the manufacture of materials used in explosives during World War I.

Advertising can also be used to "sell" to Congress members. Aircraft manufacturers prepared television commercials aimed at congressional representatives and their staff members to promote major weapons systems they wanted to build. Pat Schroeder of Colorado felt that television ads for the B-2 Stealth aircraft, a controversial fighter plane desired by the Defense Department, helped convince Congress to fund the project and saved the entire B-2 program.[13]

Another form of advertising persuades people to give their money away. Impossible? Suppose you got a letter from the St. Labre Indian School about Kevin, a toddler who had been severely burned by a space heater in his home on a Cheyenne reservation. Wouldn't it be worth a few bucks to help Kevin out?[14]

Direct-mail fund-raising is a sophisticated operation. Experts study response rates, evaluate "appeal packages," and determine which prospect lists to buy. Professional letter writers are paid an average of two thousand dollars to select just the right six hundred words to tug at contributors' heartstrings. A "guilt gift" (a small pin, address labels, envelope seals, or greeting cards) may be included to make people feel obligated to give something. The "ask," the donation requested, is often small to draw new contributors, who can be sent additional appeals later.[15] The St. Labre Indian School used an angel pin for its appeal, which was sent to more than 4 million people and brought in approximately $1 million.[16]

Two of the most successful products in American history (in terms of sales, *not* positive effect) have never been advertised. Nevertheless, they continue to have sales in the billions of dollars each year. The products are marijuana and cocaine. However, even these officially un-advertised products appear in films and on television (often in the hands of influential superstars) and are mentioned in news reports (a form of endorsement in the case of celebrity arrests). In addition, they often have promotional brand names and even logos. Street dealers provide word-of-mouth advertising and may initially offer free samples to get customers hooked.

"And Now a Word from Our Legislators": Laws and Guidelines

Advertising has never been a closely regulated industry. Early in the twentieth century, concern over product safety led to the passage of the Pure Food and Drug Act of 1906. The law forced manufacturers to list active ingredients on product labels but said nothing about advertising. Patent medicines, which had been a major target of the legislation, changed their labels but continued to make outrageous advertising claims, now adding that their products were "guaranteed" under the law.[17]

The growing threat of government regulation led to the formation of advertising clubs, which promised self-regulation. In 1911 more than one hundred such clubs adopted the phrase "Truth in Advertising," and later that year a model law proposed by a trade publication made fraudulent advertising a misdemeanor.[18] In subsequent years, advertising groups agreed on standards, created uniform rate structures, and emphasized ethics.

The Wheeler-Lea amendments to the Federal Trade Commission (FTC) Act of 1938 put a stop to "deceptive acts of commerce." This ended claims such as the one by Fleischmann's Yeast that said the product cured crooked teeth, bad skin, constipation, and halitosis (bad breath).[19]

During the 1970s the FTC and an industry group, the National Advertising Review Board, held advertising to stricter standards. The FTC ordered Listerine to spend $10 million to explain to consumers that their product will not "help prevent colds or sore throats or lessen their severity," as they had claimed.[20] Consumer protection groups also helped monitor the advertising industry.

By the late 1970s there was a growing feeling that government rules and regulations had become overly restrictive for businesses. This resulted in a trend toward deregulation, a loosening of the rules governing business, including advertising. During this period a series of Supreme Court decisions gave advertising some legal protection under the First Amendment (freedom of speech and of the press). Then, in 1980, responding to increasing support for the idea that advertising helped—not hindered—competition, Congress withdrew the FTC's power to halt "unfair" advertising and allowed it to regulate only "deceptive" ads.[21]

Advertising is still largely self-regulated by both the advertisers and the media. Liquor manufacturers, for example, have voluntarily refrained from placing ads on network television. Television networks refuse to air ads they consider offensive or inappropriate. Some advertising that is prohibited by the major television networks is accepted by cable stations. Products considered "unmentionables" by the networks but allowed on some cable stations include contraceptives, liquor, gambling, and firearms and ammunition.

Concerns about the advertising of controversial products and the use of questionable techniques to persuade buyers may or may not be justified. Meanwhile, advertising has become part of the fabric of our daily lives. Some critics worry that it is advertising's large role in our society—not the content of the advertising itself—that should be of the greatest concern.

3

Advertising's Role in American Culture

With no ads, who would pay for the media? The good fairy?

—Samuel Thurm, a senior vice-president of the U.S. Association of National Advertisers

Advertising's Benefits

Some people say that advertising actually makes products better because a bad product, advertised well, is a recipe for disaster. The story goes that a baker who made lousy pies (and therefore sold very few) decided to advertise. The next day his bakery was mobbed by crowds of people wanting to try his pies. Suddenly, he locked the door and put a sign up that said

31

"Sold Out of Pies." He had realized that if that many people found out that his pies were awful, he'd be ruined. "Before I advertise any more," he said, "I'll have to learn how to bake better pies"[1]

Manufacturers also have to be sure that their advertising claims are reasonably accurate. If the ad says the product fits in a lunch box, somebody better have made sure that it does. In addition, companies that have millions (or even billions) of dollars invested in a respected brand name are not likely to put that brand on an inferior product and risk losing loyal customers.

Advertising can also improve products by forcing competitors to make improvements. For example, there is no incentive for a car manufacturer to add a safety feature not required by law. However, if one company begins promoting safety in its advertising, its competitors will knock themselves out creating new safety features they can advertise.

When advertising is well targeted, it can save people time and money. A busy executive whose car lease is about to expire may find that a well-timed promotional package from a local car dealer offering a discount on a lease for a similar size and type of car is a welcome time-saver. The same package delivered to someone who doesn't drive or to someone who just bought a car is simply a nuisance.

Advertising can lower costs. It informs the public of a product's availability and thereby increases sales. If more products are sold, then more must be manufactured. If a greater number of products are manufactured, then the cost per item drops and the product can be sold cheaper.

Advertising lets you try products to decide for yourself. When a new product is released, advertisers often distribute free samples or inexpensive trial-size versions of the product to allow the public to sample them. They may also offer rebates, discount coupons, or other promotions.

The most beautiful thing that ever happened to horsepower

It steals the show wherever you go—the long, clean, powerful 1958 Edsel

Advertising cannot solve every problem. Despite a massive advertising campaign, sales of Edsels were disappointing and the car was discontinued.

Advertising agencies sometimes provide free or reduced-cost services to charitable organizations. Through the Advertising Council, cooperating advertising agencies produce public service ads for a wide range of government and charitable causes.

Without advertising, consumers would have to buy every program on television. Pay-per-view would be the rule, not the exception. Magazines and newspapers would cost several times what they do today.

Advertising also helps charitable organizations, educational institutions, health care organizations, and social activist groups encourage people to donate money, volunteer their efforts, or vote to change laws.

Advertising has some good aspects, but do ads ever *really* do people good? Humorist Mark Twain told a tall tale about a man who sat in front of a village hotel reading his newspaper. He saw an ad for a patent medicine that read "Cut this out. It may save your life." He clipped the ad and, through the hole where it had been, noticed an enemy sneaking up on him with a knife. He dropped the paper and successfully defended himself. *There* was an ad, Twain remarked, that really saved a man's life.[2]

Few ads have such a direct positive effect. It could, however, be argued that ads discouraging drug use, smoking, or unsafe sex have saved lives.

The Power of Advertising over Editorial

In the early days of television, advertisers sponsored individual shows and directly controlled the content of "their" shows. Camel cigarettes, for example, sponsored a news program. The company did not allow any film in which a No Smoking sign could be seen and forbade anyone to be shown smoking a cigar (except British prime minister Winston Churchill).[3]

Even today some media exist mainly as vehicles for commercial messages—the editorial [content] is there strictly to draw the audience. A special section on gardening in the local newspaper, for example, features a few articles on horticulture and dozens of ads from nurseries, gardening supply stores, and lawn and garden care companies. This *service journalism* (editorial themes, such as travel, computers, food, and fashion, designed to appeal to advertisers) has enabled magazines and newspapers to increase their revenues dramatically. Yet the goal of service journalism is not to inform (the goal of traditional journalism) as much as it is to motivate the reader to buy.

In some cases "articles" may simply be *press releases* provided by the companies. An article on nail care, for example, may stress the need for cuticle remover, nail conditioner, base polish, enamel, top coat, buffers, and other products marketed by the company that prepared the "article." While such material can be helpful, it certainly falls outside the ethics of traditional journalism, which require reporters to disclose any personal or financial connections with the subject matter. Yet an advertising executive with the *Wyoming Tribune-Eagle* newspaper defends the use of company-provided news items: "Products that are usable by the public are news," he says.[4]

Advertising or Editorial?

Advertorials are sections that, by imitating the style and format of the magazine or newspaper, appear to be regular parts of the publication rather than ads. They generally include a mix of "articles" and advertising, but the entire package has been supplied by the advertiser. Newspapers and magazines usually identify such material as advertising at the top of each page.

Consumers usually cannot tell when an editorial item has been supplied by advertisers. According to Peter Verbeck, an executive at Ogilvy and Mather, a large advertising agency, "people are five times more likely to read editorial [content] than ads."[5] And although Verbeck didn't say it, people are more inclined to *believe* what they think is editorial material as well.

"News" items provided by companies are also used by television stations. Short videotaped segments announce medical breakthroughs, new products, or company changes in ways that seem newsworthy. In an effort to avoid a canned or artificially prepared look, the companies may even supply "vanishing interviewer" tapes, which are formatted in a way that allows the stations to insert tape of their own reporters asking questions, to which the experts appear to respond.

Of even more concern is the influence of advertisers over the selection of editorial material. Sometimes advertisers object to stories critical of their products. In other cases, they may threaten to withdraw advertising when the editorial material contains sexual themes, violence, or sensitive subjects. Although some people say this results in censorship and the loss of thought-provoking programming that may offend only a small portion of the audience, others say that the practice encourages the networks to be more selective in what they air and more conscious of audience sensibilities.

Magazines have been accused of bowing to the pressures of cigarette advertisers by turning down articles on tobacco-related illness, and some studies have supported that charge. A study published in *The New England Journal of Medicine* found that women's magazines that did not carry cigarette advertising were 2.3 times more likely to cover the risks of smoking than were those that did accept such advertising.[6] A study published in the British medical journal *The Lancet* showed the same pattern among women's magazines in Great Britain.[7]

Ms. magazine dealt with the problem of advertiser influence over editorial by eliminating all advertising. Robin Morgan, editor of *Ms.* magazine, said that "*Ms.*'s content was freed enormously when we jettisoned advertising—freed in terms of health and all other coverage."[8]

Advertiser control of editorial content on television may reach a new level under a plan introduced by Harmony Entertainment. The idea is to produce TV programming that has direct input from advertisers. For example, a TV show with a western theme might, in reality, be designed to sell a particular car. "I'm just taking a 60-second commercial and making it into a long-form program," says Harmony president Warren

Weideman. The objective, according to Weideman, is "seamless advertising."[9]

Life in a 30-Second Universe

American life has changed considerably since the 1920s. The mobility provided by the automobile meant that people went places, ate out, and spent time away from their families. They also began to notice what products others were buying. Women no longer simply relied on their mothers and grandmothers, they looked to women's magazines (and the advertising they contained) for advice. Instead of determining for themselves what products they needed, people began to rely on others to tell them what they should have. Advertising became a way for companies to influence people's product selection.

Companies became concerned that their markets would become saturated, that people would own everything they wanted. What would happen, automakers worried, when everyone owned a car?

The answer was to move consumers from products that simply performed a function to those that had style. Cars began to come in colors other than black, towels in colors other than white. In 1927 General Motors began changing the body style of their cars each year. Companies discovered that by making consumers dissatisfied with what they had, they could make them buy more.[10]

People were able to compare what they had to what others had, and it seemed that there might be a way to buy into a better lifestyle. Envy began to drive purchases, and advertisers were happy to reinforce the need to "keep up with the Joneses."[11]

Critics say that advertising promotes a materialistic view of life in which the winners use the right products, know the top brands, and own the best stuff. It is this lifestyle that creates waste, depletes resources, and spoils the environment. Americans spend more money than anyone else on the planet, according to *American Demographics* magazine. By 2005, they are expected to be spending more than $7 trillion a year.[12]

Advertising promotes other values that aren't so good. Sexism is often, if not actively promoted, given a wink and a smile. Children telling cute lies, adults pulling one over on their spouses, and people being greedy and self-indulgent fill advertisements, legitimizing behaviors once frowned on or at least not bragged about.

Advertising tells people that the answer to their problems is immediate and can be bought. Within thirty seconds a character with a headache is cured, an unmarried woman meets the man of her dreams (with the help of a diet program), and a marriage is rekindled through the right choice of coffees. People can indulge themselves with fast foods, fatty snacks, and nutrition-free drinks and still be healthy and attractive.

Some say that advertising doesn't manipulate society so much as mirror it. The themes of materialism, sexuality, jealousy, greed, and vanity seen in ads are simply common motivations of American life. Ask yourself which came first: Americans' desire for more and more products to make them sexy, popular, successful, and odor-free or the companies' need to boost their own sales?

Making What's Bad for You Look Good

Early cigarette ads made claims such as "Retain slender figures," "More doctors smoke Camels," and "Your mouth feels cleaner, your throat refreshed." According to the ads, cigarettes aided digestion, calmed nerves, and best of all, made men more manly, women more sexy, and everybody more successful.

Today, health claims are prohibited; in fact, cigarette advertisements must carry grim warnings. It is hard to imagine a cigarette company today getting away with connecting cigarettes and good health. Yet look at the ads carefully: robust cowboys, people on speedboats with fresh air whipping through their hair, and slogans such as "Alive with pleasure." And until public opinion changed, many ads also featured celebrities such as John Wayne (who later died from lung cancer) who were known for their rugged personas.

Since the 1960s, when cigarette advertising came under real scrutiny, restrictions about where and how to advertise cigarettes have become increasingly tighter. In 1971 the Cigarette Act banned cigarette advertising on radio and television in the United States. In 1997 cities such as San Francisco, Baltimore, and New York passed ordinances to ban tobacco advertising on billboards, vehicles, bus shelters, and other public places.

Following a number of lawsuits won by individual states trying to recover the costs of treating tobacco-related illnesses, Congress attempted to strike a national settlement with the tobacco industry. The proposed agreement—which would have prohibited advertising characters such as Joe Camel and banned billboard ads, imprinted clothing, and sponsorship of sporting events—was voted down. Additional restrictions on cigarette advertising aren't expected to go into effect until late 1999.[13] In the interim, tobacco manufacturers are working to sway public opinion against further legislation through . . . advertising.

In 1997 Europe's health ministers signed an agreement to ban most cigarette ads by 2006. Television and radio ads are already banned in Europe, but the new plan would also eliminate cigarette advertising on billboards, magazines, newspapers, and even clothing.[14]

The tobacco industry has successfully overcome government restrictions time and time again. "Trying to contain this industry," says Rick Pollay of the University of British Columbia, "is like making a balloon smaller by squeezing it."[15] The companies are beginning to develop symbols or words that convey the product, preparing for a day when companies may be forbidden to even mention the product's name.

Alcohol Advertising

Advertising of alcoholic beverages has also come under fire. The industry has been criticized for targeting both underage and heavy drinkers. A small percentage of drinkers consume the largest proportion of alcohol. Advertisements that encourage daytime drinking, the use of alcohol to reduce stress or promote psychological well-being, or the drinking of alcohol as an escape from problems give the heavy drinker an excuse to drink even more. Slogans such as "The one beer to have when you're having more than one" and "Any time is Miller time" give the impression that heavy drinking is normal.

Both tobacco and alcohol advertisers say that ads do not push use of their product, they simply attempt to persuade people who use the product to choose their brand. Critics say that this is nonsense. They point out that advertising encourages the use of almost every other kind of product, so why wouldn't it do the same for alcohol and tobacco?

Alcohol and tobacco companies claim that if restrictions are allowed on their products based on the harm they cause, it will only be a matter of time before many other products come under similar controls: automobiles, fatty foods, sugary cereals, and so forth. In addition, they say, restrictions wouldn't work. As James Kuras of McCann-Erickson advertising agency in New York says: "Trying to control drunk drivers by outlawing the advertising of alcohol makes as little sense as trying to control the Ku Klux Klan by outlawing bed linens."[16]

Packaging the Candidate

In 1964 a television commercial aired—but just once. It showed a little girl in a field of daisies, picking petals one by one. A voice with a Russian accent counted down to zero, at which point an explosion obliterated the scene. A voice then explained, to an audience already concerned about the possibility of nuclear war, the dangers of confrontation with the Soviet Union. It was an ad supporting Lyndon B. Johnson for president. Without ever saying so, the ad suggested that Johnson's opponent, Barry Goldwater, was trigger-happy and might bring on a nuclear holocaust.[17] Even though the ad was withdrawn following protests, the point had been made, and more than thirty years later, many people still remember that ad.

Political advertisements are brilliant in their ability to communicate messages that go to the heart of the voters' fears. A 1990 ad for Senator Jesse Helms of North Carolina showed a white man's hands tearing up a notice informing him that he had not gotten a job (because the company had to hire a minority, the voice-over intoned). The idea that white men were losing jobs to African-American men played to the fears of white voters.

Television has revolutionized political campaigns. The televised debate between Kennedy and Nixon in 1960 may have affected the election by turning voters away from the sweating, uncomfortable Nixon and toward the handsome, self-assured Kennedy. Today political candidates are groomed and coached like movie stars, and elections have become a battle of the wallets. Candidates with small budgets have virtually no chance of being elected.

Political advertising has become increasingly

focused on the opponent's shortcomings rather than the candidate's own record or the issues involved in the campaign. By the 1988 presidential election, an estimated 70 percent of ads were classified as negative.[18] The 1992 Senate campaigns were so negative that an estimated 6 million voters stayed home in disgust.[19] Politicians are affected as well. Senator

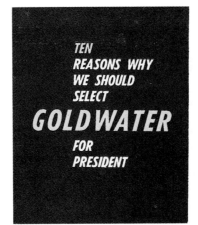

WHY WE NEED SEN. BARRY GOLDWATER

1. Barry Goldwater is the unifying force for the GOP—the single most popular man in all sections of the country, north, south, east and west.

2. Barry Goldwater is an experienced lawmaker with 11 years service in the United States Senate, our Nation's most important legislative body.

3. Barry Goldwater has traveled widely and is a widely acclaimed expert in foreign affairs who will lead the Free World to greater unity and resolution in the Cold War.

4. Barry Goldwater is a fiscal conservative who believes in a balanced budget and a tax structure which will promote economic growth and individual initiative.

5. Barry Goldwater is a staunch defender of personal freedom and the rights of every American, regardless of race, creed or color.

6. Barry Goldwater is a practical businessman who successfully managed a business and met a payroll, even during the Depression.

7. Barry Goldwater is a World War II veteran and jet pilot—presently a major general in the U. S. Air Reserve—who knows we must remain militarily strong.

8. Barry Goldwater is a man devoted to his family, with a lovely wife and four children.

9. Barry Goldwater is an extraordinary all-American man — author, explorer, linguist, historian, pilot, photographer, "ham" radio operator, and athlete.

10. Barry Goldwater is a dedicated Party man who will actively support every Republican running for office at the local, state and Federal levels.

BARRY GOLDWATER IS THE REPUBLICAN OPPORTUNITY TO WIN IN 1964!

Advertising political candidates has become much more sophisticated since this print ad from 1964.

Howard Baker complained when he was leader in the Senate that he couldn't get votes on controversial issues. When he asked for support, he said fellow senators responded, "Howard, I would like to vote with you but they would kill me with negative ads next time I run."[20]

Modern presidential candidates (and incumbents) have become even more adept at working the media to their own advantage. Richard Nixon appointed H. R. Haldeman, an advertising executive, as his chief of staff. Reagan managed to sell his image on an emotional rather than intellectual level, helping to make him one of the country's most popular presidents. Clinton's ability to manipulate or spin the way news about him is portrayed in the media has been so successful that it has enabled him to resist countless accusations and scandals.

Creating false images for political purposes is nothing new. In 1840 presidential candidate William Henry Harrison was depicted as a cider-drinking farmer who lived in a log cabin, even though he lived in a mansion and owned a two-thousand-acre estate worked by tenant farmers.

The power of political advertising continues to grow. The problem is that political advertising is not like product advertising, where if consumers realize the advertising is misleading, they just won't buy the product again. If the "product" is an elected official, they may be stuck with their choice for years.

4

Getting Attention at Any Cost

It has become all too apparent that wolves are not led onto paths of righteousness by offering them the carrot of self-discipline. Wolves ignore carrots; they want meat, and they don't care how bloody it is.

—Paul Rand Dixon, chairman of the FTC, in an address to advertising executives

Breaking Through the Clutter

On September 12, 1997, a full-page advertisement appeared in the national news section of *The New York Times*. Under a stunning photograph of a baby and the headline "Children Made to Order" were the words: "At Gattaca, it is now possible to engineer your offspring."

The ad then provided a checklist to help readers decide which traits they wanted to engineer in or out of their newborns. In addition to inheritable diseases, the list included such things as skin color, height, musical ability, athletic prowess, and intellect. At the bottom of the ad appeared a Gattaca logo, a Web site address, and the words "For an appointment call 1-888-4-BEST-DNA."

The ad was a shocker. But *Gattaca* was actually a futuristic movie from Columbia Pictures.

Did it trick people? Absolutely. But, as a result, the message got through. People would now not only remember the movie but probably be able to recall what it is about.

Advertisers have always strived for the unexpected. In 1896 an elderly woman complained in a letter to *The Times* in London that she had been awakened by her maid, who clutched a telegram, the tool used to convey urgent, often tragic news. When the frightened woman opened the telegram, the message read, "Peter Robinson's sale now proceeding."[1]

Advertisers go to great lengths to break through the advertising clutter and get noticed. Junk mail is disguised as telegrams, legal documents, official government communications, bills, checks, prize notifications, and personal letters. An envelope bearing a first-class stamp (as opposed to a bulk-mail permit stamp) and what appears to be a hand-typed name and address demands opening—it could be something important.

One such mailing contained a newspaper clipping about a weight-loss product. A handwritten note on the top said, "Nancy, Try it. It works!" But it was not a helpful tip from a friend—it was an ad.

Advertisers place messages virtually anywhere they can. Advertisements now appear on shopping carts, the backs of doors in toilet stalls, fruits and vegetables, the scoreboards at sporting events, hot-air balloons, and the backs of store receipts. Commercial messages are towed by airplanes, placed in hospital waiting rooms, sent by fax, yelled through loudspeakers at public events, and written in the sky with smoke. The more unexpected the means of communication, the more likely the message will be noticed.

Advertising Goes On-Line

In 1995 advertisers spent $50 million on on-line (Internet) advertising. By 1996 the amount had risen to $200 million. Veronis, Suhler & Associates, an investment banking firm that specializes in media deals, estimates that by 2001 on-line advertising expenditures could reach $2.5 billion.[2]

Initial attempts at Internet advertising were simple banners, like billboards, that appeared at the top of the computer screen. Then came pop-up windows that intrude into the page, roadblocks (full-screen ads that users must pass to reach the site they want to access), and tickers (banner ads that appear between a moving stream of headlines at a site). *Intermercials* now provide a thirty-second animated commercial to visitors who click on the box (about 2 to 4 percent do).[3]

Other techniques are being developed all the time. Engage, a company that provides on-line games, began offering ads on "satellites" that circle a three-dimensional globe on Engage's home page. What advertisers really want, however, is to be inescapable. Interactive Imaginations recently introduced a way for full-page ads to be spread throughout a game player's path.[4]

When the Weather Channel offered a way for users to create a personalized weather page, one thousand people jumped on it in the first forty minutes. It was a terrific idea. Users could set up their page to display the maps they preferred, weather for the cities they chose, and other specific information. After all, people want to know about their own weather, not other people's. What the participants may not have realized was the ultimate result: The Weather Channel could now deliver ads to people in specific areas—allergy medications to people in areas with high pollen counts, for example. "For the first time, we know who people are," said Todd Walrath, director of product development at the Weather Channel.[5] Part of the customization process includes specifying sex, age, and interests, as well as disclosing income range—important information for potential advertisers but probably not essential to developing a customized weather map.

The ultimate goal, say many advertisers, is to use personalized information for one-on-one marketing. This *microtargeting* would give advertisers the ability to direct specific, personalized ads to particular individuals. Melissa Bane, senior analyst at the Yankee Group, calls it "the Holy Grail for advertisers."[6]

In the future, advertisers hope to know everything about you and to present you with offers you are highly likely to act on. It would be the equivalent of having your own personal sales representative who knows what you want and how to make you buy it. What's wrong with that?

Concerns About Information Gathering

Some people worry about all the information being collected and exchanged via the Internet. Already, some sites can detect your general location. They can also see the last few sites you have visited. Following this *clickstream*, or "mouse droppings" as some refer to it, allows marketers to learn about your interests without your knowing it.

Through the use of *cookies* (small files that Web publishers can save onto your computer either permanently or temporarily), they can recognize who you are, what capabilities your computer has, which ads you've been shown, and what preferences you have indicated in the past. Marketers say this allows them to recognize you, saving time and assuring your needs are met.

Due to the objections raised by privacy advocates, some browsers now offer the user the option to reject cookies, and others may block cookies entirely. There are also programs available that can "anonymize" users.

Although one might think microtargeting would

result in fewer ads, the fact is that this capability will open the door to thousands of smaller companies that will now be able to afford advertising on the Internet because they can target just the people in their area.

E-mail has also become a popular marketing tool. People who sign up to have customized newsletters, movie reviews, or other information sent to their e-mail addresses make good advertising targets because they have already shown what kinds of things interest them. Advertisers are expected to spend $1 billion by the year 2002 to reach customers by e-mail.[7]

At the opposite end of the spectrum is *spam*, automated mailings of unsolicited commercial e-mail messages sent to thousands, even millions, of people. "DON'T LET THIS BE THE MOST EXPENSIVE MISTAKE OF YOU [sic] LIFE!! READ ON!!" screams an e-mail message describing a scheme for getting rich by using an e-mail version of a chain letter.[8]

Spam has become quite a problem, particularly for people on popular Internet providers such as America Online. On some days spam accounts for as much as 30 percent of the 8 to 9 million e-mail messages that go through America Online, according to vice-president and general counsel George Vradenburg.[9]

Such massive amounts of e-mail bog down the Internet and can cause computer crashes. It has become such a problem that several bills to ban or regulate junk e-mail have been introduced in Congress, and many states are considering legislation as well. The Federal Trade Commission has commissioned a study to help determine what to do about the problem.

The tobacco and alcohol industries have discovered the unique opportunity the Internet holds for advertising. Their sites tend to glamorize drinking and smoking. Some are connected with prosmoking organizations such as the National Smokers Alliance and the American Smokers Alliance, groups that have financial ties to tobacco companies. Sites often contain photographs of celebrities smoking or drinking, interactive environments where "hip" people hang out, rock music audio clips, free screensavers, logo-imprinted merchandise offers, and chat rooms. The chat is often laced with subtle commercial messages (with no warnings required) and frequently have an "us (the cool) vs. them (the uncool)" attitude that appeals to a young person's need for acceptance. "This plugs right into the adolescent market," says Michael Brody, a child psychiatrist, "where appearing cool and sense of identity are based on belonging."[10]

The Art of Deception

Sometimes ads are clearly *deceptive*; other times they are simply misleading. "Never more than a gram of sodium," bragged an ad for Stouffer's Lean Cuisine, when sodium is measured in milligrams of salt, and at up to nine hundred milligrams, the frozen dinners were jam-packed. A lite sausage from Swift Premium was promoted as 76 percent fat-free. True. However, that means it contained 24 percent fat—a cardiac nightmare.[11] Ivory soap was touted "so pure it floats," when in fact, it floated because it contained more air (and therefore less soap) than other products.

One of the most common forms of deception in advertising is the lie of omission (leaving out a critical piece of information). This can be seen in advertisements for movies. A quote such as "Don James is clearly the best!" might be used in a newspaper ad, followed by the name of a well-known movie critic. What the critic may actually have said is: "This movie stinks. The cast consists of an abominable assortment of hacks, among whom Don James is clearly the best."

Ads can be misleading and even deceptive, but some people say that advertising can also cause real harm. In the 1970s American manufacturers were promoting a breast-milk substitute (formula) in Third World countries through advertising, free samples, and inducements for medical workers. Poor women in developing countries bought the expensive formula (rather than breast-feed their babies with free, medically superior breast milk), then diluted it too much (to make it go further) with water that was often contaminated. The result was malnutrition, illness, and in some cases, death. The companies involved protested that they were responding only to demand for infant formula, not creating it, and that their formula was better than the combinations of water, sugar, flour, and root extracts the women used before their marketing efforts. As a result of pressure by health organizations and a consumer boycott in the

Advertising claims are now more carefully controlled, particularly those for medical products.

United States, however, the companies changed their marketing practices.[12]

Deceptive Advertising IQ Test

Advertisers go to great lengths to make their products look good. A few go too far. See if you can guess why the following advertisements were questioned:

1. A chain of drugstores advertised that their products were approved by the Consumer Protective Institute and had earned the CPI Seal.[13]

2. An ad for canned soup pictured a bowl chock-full of vegetables.[14]

3. Shaving cream was shown to have such "super-moisturizing power" that it could shave sandpaper.[15]

4. Ads for a glass company showed the company's car window glass and house window glass to be completely free of distortion.[16]

Answers are on page 124.

5

New and Improved Ways to Make You Buy

Why is the merchant who doesn't advertise like a man in a rowboat?
Because he has to get along without sales.

—advertising joke from 1901

Product Comparisons

Although it would seem that comparing products side by side would help consumers make informed buying decisions, advertising agencies and trade groups discouraged direct product comparisons during the 1960s, because they feared their own products might be portrayed unfairly by the competition. Comparisons also raised the frightening prospect that a small, upstart company could show that its product was as good (or better) than the products made by the bigger companies. The television networks even banned comparative ads for a time (NBC dropped its ban in 1964), but in 1972 the FTC claimed such restrictions were restraining trade and pressured the networks to end the ban. By 1980 one in four commercials on ABC television was a product comparison.[1] Today, product comparisons are common, particularly for pain relievers, cars, and detergents.[2]

Some product comparison campaigns were legendary. When the makers of 7-Up wanted a share of Coke's market, they dubbed their product "the Uncola." When Pepsi also started to eat away at Coke's business, the Coca-Cola Company responded by saying of Coke: "It's the real thing." Pepsi answered with a series of blind taste tests against Coke that doubled Pepsi's market share within a year.[3]

The best-known comparisons are probably the ads for weight-loss products that use before and after pictures to show the dramatic results. In an infamous case, the makers of Regimen tablets claimed the product produced weight loss without dieting. Dorothy Bryce, a model for the before and after photos, testified that she had lost weight by living on black coffee, tranquilizers, and a thyroid extract. The company was brought to trial for violating government Food and Drug Administration regulations. A man who worked for the agency that produced the ad campaign gave this excuse: "Thousands of other advertisers and agencies are doing the same kind of thing. We just happen to be the fall guys that the government picked on."[4]

Sometimes comparisons aren't really comparisons. A huge corporation with dozens of brands may compare one to another in an ad without ever acknowledging that they make both products. Or what is hailed as a feature may, in fact, be something all brands share. For example, one company claimed that its beer bottles were "washed with live steam," as all beer bottles are.

Nine out of Ten Doctors Recommend . . .

On the radio, disk jockeys chat about a local restaurant. "Have you tried the chicken in pastry?" asks one. "Yeah, that's great but have you had the spinach salad? It's to die for." Sounds like normal DJ chitchat, but it is actually an advertisement. A company has paid for a specific period of time during which their restaurant will be promoted by the on-air personalities. This type of advertising can be very powerful. It is often undetected. It creates a sense that the product being discussed is something hot and new and that the listener should get in on it. Exaggerations that the advertiser itself could never get away with slip by because the commercials are done live and change each time.

Endorsements are a way for advertisers to buy credibility for their products. A company selling a theft-protection product may hire an actor known for portraying a police officer on television. A drug company marketing a pain reliever may choose someone who has played a doctor on a drama series. Both are actors; neither is an authority qualified to lend advice on crime prevention or medical care. They were hired because they give people the *impression* that they are qualified.

The interesting thing about endorsements is that people believe them, even when there is considerable doubt that the endorser actually likes or uses the product. In 1986 Pepsi paid singer Michael Jackson nearly $15 million to appear in two television commercials and consult on a third. Jackson would not be shown drinking, or even holding, the product. In fact, many people knew that, as a Jehovah's Witness, Jackson did not consume caffeine and so never drank Pepsi. Yet the company felt that his connection with Pepsi, even for only 180 seconds of airtime, was worth paying him many times more than the price top movie stars were commanding for full-length films.[5]

Attention Please!

One way advertisers increase the numbers of people seeing their ads is through *borrowed interest*. Research has shown, for example, that babies grab attention, so many advertisers use babies in their advertising, even if their product has nothing at all to do with babies or children. An ad with the headline "Baby Your Legs" showed a woman holding an adorable baby. The baby got the reader to stop and read the ad to see what it was about (a shaver for women).

Advertisers also try to borrow interest from

current events: medical breakthroughs, world news, and major events. At the close of the Gulf War, NYNEX telecommunications aired an ad featuring a montage of soldiers in the desert, women at home watching war planes on TV, a soldier on the phone, and other images, followed by a shot of planet earth. "Never is information more crucial to democracy than at times like these," read the text, as it rolled down the screen followed by the NYNEX logo. The viewer would think that NYNEX was a really crucial player in international communications during the Gulf War. Yet as a company that owned only local

Today's advertising often involves dramatic stories in which the product may not even be mentioned but still plays a role in the story. Levi Strauss & Co. built an ad for Levi's® Jeans around a grocery clerk's fantasy.

telephone companies, such as New York Telephone and New England Telephone, NYNEX wasn't even allowed to provide long-distance calls, let alone international ones. But the company did have some overseas holdings and wanted to project a global image.[6]

Another technique advertisers use to get attention is contests. Few people can resist the allure of easy money. Advertisers know this. Contests are used to get people to read advertising material, to get people's names and addresses for mailing lists, and to get people to buy products. Although it is illegal to require a purchase in order to enter a contest or to show preference to entrants who purchase products, people often get the idea (which advertisers don't discourage) that they have a better chance of winning if they buy a magazine, use the special coupon that comes with the product, or get the "official entry blank" from the store. While what is promoted is the contest, the advertiser's goal is to get your money (or at least your name and address).

Targeting Women and Minorities

When advertisers realized that women were the major purchasers of many products, they began to make their pitch directly to women. An ad from the 1920s states, "What does a man know about complexion, the skin? Nothing. . . . You, the woman of the family, understand what the care of the skin means."[7]

In the days before marketers caught on to the fact that African Americans, Hispanics, gays, and other

minorities actually bought products like everyone
else, advertising often promoted outrageous stereotypes. An ad for Aunt Jemima Pancakes (its name and
logo reminiscent of a slavery-era "mammy") carried
the phrase "Folks sho' whoops with joy over Aunt
Jemima Pancakes." A Fritos corn chip campaign featured a Mexican "bandito" caricature, complete with
mustache and sombrero. Gay and lesbian consumers
were generally just ignored (as were the disabled and,
to some extent, the elderly).

The first attempts to cater to black consumers were
simply to mix a few token African Americans into the
backgrounds of commercials. Advertisers later began
to feature African Americans in commercials but in a
way that prompted Thomas Burrell, founder of Burrell
Advertising of Chicago, a black-owned advertising
agency, to remark, "Black people are not dark-skinned
white people."[8] Burrell suggested that African
Americans have different cultural values and should be
approached as black consumers.

Companies that market products with strong
sales among African-American consumers soon began
actively promoting their products directly to this
audience. In 1967 African Americans appeared in
only 5 percent of all TV ads. By 1976 the figure had
risen to 13 percent.[9] Now, many companies produce
ads specifically for African-American audiences.

Companies have been criticized for exploiting the
African-American community by promoting products
such as malt liquor and cigarettes in urban black
neighborhoods. Studies in Baltimore and other cities
have found that 75 percent of the billboards in black

NO DINNER?

Early ads depicted minorities using insulting stereotypes designed to be funny to a white audience.

neighborhoods advertise tobacco and alcohol, and minorities suffer disproportionately from death and disease resulting from these products.[10] A study in California found that 64 percent of the billboards in minority communities were promoting tobacco, more than double the national average.[11] In some cases, the advertising even glamorizes the violent aspects of inner-city life with slogans such as "It'll blow you away" and "Too cold to hold, bold like Smith & Wesson" (St. Ides Malt Liquor).[12]

Documents released by the tobacco industry in 1998 showed that cigarette companies intentionally targeted black consumers. A 1973 Brown & Williamson document showed that the company spent 17 percent of its promotional budget on marketing to African Americans (at a time when that group made up only about 10 percent of the population). A 1977 promotion plan for Kool cigarettes recommended giving out basketballs in Kool brand colors. "The green and white ball could become an interesting symbol within the inner city and could be very popular," the document said.[13]

Advertisers differ in how they approach gay and lesbian consumers. Some entirely avoid magazines and newspapers for gay audiences. Some run mainstream ads in gay media. Others create ambiguous ads, such as the Volkswagen television ad that showed two men driving around with a discarded chair. While the pair seemed like a couple to gay viewers, most heterosexuals took them to be friends.[14] A few, like Subaru, create ads specifically for a gay audience with obviously gay or (in the case of Subaru) lesbian characters. Most advertisers still avoid placing gay-oriented ads in nongay media, however.

Advertisers now often tailor their ads to specific audiences. They may have several versions of the same ad with only minor changes to make it more appealing to a particular market segment. With the increasing fragmentation of American society and the growing competition for each group's pocketbook, advertising to specialized markets will probably continue to grow for some time.

Advertising's Little White Lies

If you've ever wondered why the food you make at home never looks quite as good as it does in the advertisements, meet today's food stylist. Food stylists are artists who use food as their medium. They paint carrots with glycerin to make them shine, glue rice into perfect mounds, put plastic cubes in glasses to simulate ice, use doughs made to look like ice cream, and place each and every sesame seed on those perfect-looking hamburger buns. The result is a carefully contrived "reality."

Products look and act better in advertising than in real life. Advertised products easily remove "dirt" that may be nothing more than powdered graphite. Models with small hands make products look larger. Professional drivers operate cars under perfect conditions.

Color, lighting, music, and special effects are all used to create an image, stimulate emotions, or appeal to subconscious desires. A scene for a pain remedy may start with a murky, black-and-white image of a woman holding her head. The music is loud and vaguely irritating. Then the star (the product) is produced. The scene lightens, the music brightens, and the woman makes a miracle recovery. Even what the models wear has been chosen carefully to convey a certain feeling or idea. Ads for women's sanitary products, for example, nearly always feature women wearing white.

"Scientific studies" are a way to buy legitimacy for a product. Such studies may be nothing more than surveys conducted by the company's advertising agency. Unlike real scientific research, any results that do not support the advertiser's claims are simply thrown out. The "research" is often primarily a hunt to find some area of superiority that can be promoted.

The exception to this is medical and pharmaceutical advertising, which is more tightly regulated due to the health implications. Initially, the Food and Drug Administration (FDA) did not allow manufacturers to advertise prescription drugs directly to consumers. What few ads appeared never even mentioned the drug's name. In 1997 the FDA began to allow manufacturers to name both the product and the condition it treats in ads directed to consumers. Surveys showed the public approved of the ads and paid attention to them. Final rules detailing what the drug companies could and couldn't say in ads were expected to be issued at the end of 1998.[15]

Some claims are hard to pin down. "Makes your hair feel stronger." Stronger than what? Why does your hair need to feel strong? These are the kinds of claims that sound good and do not have to be defended because they are basically meaningless.

Playing with Your Mind

In the 1980s Isuzu ads confronted growing audience distrust with "Joe Isuzu," a smarmy salesman whose outrageous claims were countered with printed captions such as "Sounds like a lie." The ads were funny, lowered sales resistance, and sold cars.

Letting the audience behind the scenes is a way to disarm skeptical viewers. This technique was used in a Nike commercial directed by Spike Lee and starring Michael Jordan. Lee was seen interrupting his

Companies no longer rely on stereotypes or token minorities in their advertising. This ad by Levi Strauss & Co. was one of a series that featured funky urban stories to promote Levi's®.

own commercial to yell to noisy neighbors, "Shut up! I'm doing a Nike commercial here."[16] Another example of an advertising campaign that mocked itself was the Sprite "Image Is Nothing, Obey Your Thirst" campaign. The print ad copy included the statement, "But you probably know all this already because every ad and magazine has told you a *zillion* times." By having an antiadvertising tone, the marketers hoped to appeal to teenagers.[17]

Advertisers have also tried to overcome skepticism by going for the heart rather than the brain. They create scenes of reunited loved ones, children hugging their mothers, and underdogs achieving despite all odds. These stories play to the deepest emotional holes in all of us—holes that can be filled with products. The goal is to create the kind of bond between the consumer and the product that establishes long-term brand loyalty. The advertiser hopes that the consumer doesn't pause as their teary eyes begin to clear and say, "Now what did that have to do with toilet cleanser again?"

Think you're too cool to fall for such manipulation? Advertisers are ready for you. They pitch products differently to young people, because kids reared on television have grown up doubting advertising. They let you know that they realize you are too cool to fall for an advertising claim. Then they tell you that you are so cool, you are cool enough to want their product.

Whether you know it or not, advertisers observe, study, and analyze you like laboratory rats. They conduct studies to determine what you want to be called ("young men/women"), which trends are safe for marketers to use (baggy clothes, caring about the environment) and which are not (the word "dude", bell-bottoms), even what type of setting teens prefer to see in ads (beaches).[18]

Advertisers also know how to push the conformity button. The main theme of most advertising is "Join us and become unique."[19] How else can you explain the ad for Nice 'n Easy hair coloring that showed a woman boasting, "It lets me be me"?

6

Targeting Kids

In the past, we've targeted the moms. Now we're targeting the kids.

—Colleen Rizzo, Carlson & Partners
advertising agency

The Spending Power of Kids

Kids fourteen and under spend an estimated $20 billion a year and influence purchases by parents, grandparents, and others to the tune of $200 billion a year.[1] As a result, advertisers spend big bucks to reach kids: an estimated $800 million for ads on children's television programs alone.[2]

Experts say that children are particularly vulnerable to the persuasive effects of

69

advertising, especially television commercials, because they lack the skills and the experiences necessary to analyze advertising messages. Their openess makes them all the more appealing to advertisers. "Kids are the most pure consumers you could have," says Debra McMahon, a vice-president at Mercer Management Consulting. "They tend to interpret your ad literally. They are infinitely open."[3]

In the 1960s advertisers began to recognize the potential profits to be made from the youth market and began to target advertising directly at children. But by the 1970s concern grew about the power of such appeals. A group of women in Boston formed a group called Action for Children's Television (ACT). ACT succeeded in stopping vitamin advertising to children, banning the use of hosts or stars of programs making pitches, prohibiting commercials that urged children to ask their parents to buy products, and outlawing the practice of exaggerating the size or speed of toys.

ACT was also able to get limits placed on the number of ads that could air during weekend children's shows. Even so, children see at least an hour of television commercials for every five hours of programs they watch.[4]

Advertisers no longer feel any hesitation in approaching children directly. Mailings feature engaging graphics or characters and offer free gifts or discounts. If the child has registered a product, joined a club, subscribed to a magazine, or given marketing information on the Internet, mailings may be remarkably on-target to the child's age and interests.

Do advertising messages get through to kids? The answer seems to be an emphatic yes, even for very young children. When *American Demographics* magazine asked 112 children aged eight to ten to "draw what comes to mind when you think about going shopping," the children drew specific brands in twenty of the thirty-eight categories of products they pictured themselves buying. In one case, a third grader correctly spelled the brand name Esprit (including the open E used in the logo) but misspelled the words *shirts* and *skirts*.[5]

It's All in the Merchandise

In 1983, *He-Man and the Masters of the Universe* appeared on television. Kids seemed to love the program and in just three years bought more than 70 million plastic figures based on the series. What the kids didn't know was that the plastic figures actually came first. *He-Man* was the first of many shows to be developed and controlled by toy companies.

By 1986 there were more than sixty shows that were basically half-hour toy commercials. The *G.I. Joe* series alone included ninety half-hour shows showcasing the characters, vehicles, and weapons kids could buy at their local toy store.[6] It was a brilliant and extremely successful marketing idea. The toy companies brought a huge audience to the television broadcasters, and the television programs provided a fortune in tantalizing promotion for their products.

Toy-based shows triggered protests from several sides. Competing toy companies (if they didn't have

Levi Strauss invented jeans in the 1800s, when gold miners needed sturdy pants. Later, jeans became a fashion item.

their own shows) called them unfair. Action for Children's Television called them insidious, and even advertising trade magazines expressed discomfort. In an editorial, *Advertising Age* called the practice "a TV license to steal from kids."[7]

Today, licensed characters continue to be big business. Even public broadcasting has gotten into the action. Store sales of *Sesame Street* characters alone bring in an estimated $1 billion a year.[8]

"Kids, Tell Mom"

A roadside ice-cream stand in Pennsylvania has a sign that says "Scream Until Dad Stops." Although humorous, the idea of encouraging children to hound their parents into buying things is well known to advertisers. The child as in-house salesperson is a powerful friend to advertisers.

There was a time when it was considered taking unfair advantage to appeal to the immature judgment of children. Products were advertised to parents, who decided what their children wore, ate, watched, and played with. Today, advertisers count on the "pestering factor" and sell directly to kids.

How many ten-year-old kids can spring for a Chevy minivan? Probably not many. Yet a two-page ad for the vehicle appeared in *Sports Illustrated for Kids*, a publication with an audience of eight- to fourteen-year-olds. The product's brand manager, Karen Francis, calls the group "back-seat consumers" and said that parents had told her that their kids had often cast the tie-breaking vote in family car-buying decisions.[9] "Ten years ago, it was cereal, candy, and toys. Today, it's also computers and airlines and hotels and banks," according to Julie Halpin, general manager of Saatchi & Saatchi Advertising's Kid Connection division.[10]

One positive outgrowth of all the interest in advertising to children is the proliferation of new magazines, Web sites, television shows, even entire TV channels for kids. *Time*, *Sports Illustrated*, *People*, and other publications have started children's versions of their magazines. Of course, most of the new child-oriented media contain advertising, increasing the ad-overload kids already experience.

Step into My Web

Spinning cookies, flashing lights, and a playground of colorful graphics, games, and fun—Welcome to the

"Nabisco® Kids Home Page" section of Nabisco's Web site at <www.nabisco.com>. "Way cool!" the introduction reads,

> You made it to BITE AFTER BYTE—the site that's really an awesome cyberspace adventure! This is *Nabisco Thing's World*—where you can fly through time, speak your mind and hang out with your buds. You're in control and you've got the Nabisco Thing™ along for the ride. So plug in and taste the excitement—It's total wow!

Here, kids can find out how to win a busload of toys and cookies, buy clothing and accessories featuring Nabisco brand logos, play a game in which they try to save the world from "the totally uncool Dr. Snackmasher," and provide "back talk" by answering questions in exchange for a Chips Ahoy! screensaver.

Do most kids understand the purpose of this Web site? Aside from the obvious product promotion and direct sales of merchandise, Nabisco (like many other companies) uses it to collect valuable marketing data. The questions posed in the "Back Talk" area are framed in the context of letting kids speak their minds. But questions such as "What snacks do you think are cool?" and "What is your favorite TV show?" provide direction on which new products to develop, where to place television commercials, and even how to advertise products so that kids will want to buy them. Is that a small price to pay for a fun, free, and relatively harmless Web site for kids? Officials for Nabisco say the site, which changes frequently, draws between fifteen thousand and twenty-five thousand visitors a day. When they are running a contest with a prize, they can get up to seventy-five thousand in a single day.[11]

In 1996, approximately 4 million kids under age seventeen went on-line.[12] This ready and eager audience quickly became a gold mine for companies wanting to market products to children. With no regulations to restrict the content of Web sites, they created innovative interactive environments, blending advertising, entertainment, and in some cases, education, in a seamless mix of fun and games.

In 1997, one third of the 15 million or so existing Web sites were run by corporations, and the number is growing daily.[13] And while there are certainly plenty of noncommercial sites run by libraries, museums, universities, and other institutions, the corporate cyberworlds are often much flashier and impressive to kids.

On-line environments capture children's imaginations. As Erica Gruen, director of Saatchi & Saatchi Interactive, puts it, "There is nothing else that exists like it for advertisers to build relationships with kids."[14] Kids can talk to advertising characters, play with brand logos, hear promotional jingles, watch commercial videos, and even cut, paste, and color their own advertising images. Is the ability to forge such a relationship an opportunity for advertisers or a vulnerability that shouldn't be exploited?

Criticisms of On-Line Advertising

Critics have complained about the practices some marketers use to reach kids on the Internet. Initially, some Web sites existed exclusively to gather research or develop mailing lists. Kids were offered free merchandise in exchange for personal information about themselves and their families that could be used by advertisers. Under guises such as registering for a birthday surprise, nominating a hero, joining a club, receiving a free gift, or entering a contest, the sites got kids to provide valuable information.

In April 1997 the Children's Advertising Review Unit, an industry group that seeks to promote responsibility through voluntary self-regulation rather than government legislation, issued guidelines on Internet marketing to children. The voluntary guidelines recommended that when companies ask children for information, they explain why they are asking for the information and what they will do with it.

The Clinton administration supported the idea of self-regulation. President Clinton's senior adviser for policy development, Ira Magaziner, said, "People say: 'You're just being a shill. You're leaving the Internet open to let industry do all this terrible marketing to children.'" He explained that the administration was responding to a larger fear: the fear that governments would "overregulate, overtax and overcensor the Internet and strangle development."[15]

Most advertisers are now aware of parents' concerns and are careful to clearly identify advertising messages. Nabisco, for example, uses "Ad Break," a movie clapboard character, and tells kids that when they see the character "it means you are viewing a commercial message designed to sell you something." Nabisco also reminds children under eighteen to get their parents' permission before leaving any information or trying to buy anything on-line. In a separate message for parents, they spell out their policies for collecting and using marketing information.

Proponents say that there is nothing wrong with getting marketing information from children. The tradition of collecting names and addresses for marketing purposes is an old one, from encouraging kids to send cereal box tops for magic decoder rings to offering club memberships and other incentives. And children may be more savvy than adults sometimes think. "The same cognitive development that enables children to get around the Web," says John Calfee, a former staff economist with the Federal Trade Commission and now a resident scholar at the American Enterprise Institute, "also lets them recognize advertising when they see it."[16]

Targeting Teens

By the year 2005 teenagers will form a larger percentage of the population than any other age group.[17] According to *Advertising Age* magazine, teenagers spend more than $100 billion a year, 2 percent of total consumer expenditures.[18] Teenage boys spend about $68 a week ($44 of their own and $24 in family money), and teenage girls spend about $65 ($34 of their own and $31 of the family's).[19] As Peter Zollo, author of an eye-opening book written for companies wanting to sell products to teens, put it, "Teens' considerable income is almost exclusively discretionary. They are consumers with a mission: they want to spend on whatever happens to please them. What a compelling advertising target!"[20]

Advertisers target teens for other reasons as well. Teens establish buying habits they will carry into adulthood. Studies conducted for *Seventeen* magazine have shown that 29 percent of adult women still buy the brand of coffee they preferred as teenagers, and 41 percent buy the same brand of mascara. "If you miss her," the magazine warns its advertisers, "then you may miss her for ever. She's at that receptive age when her looks, tastes and brand loyalties are being established. . . . Reach a girl in her *Seventeen* years and she may be yours for life.[21]

Advertising Goes to School

Kids are bombarded with advertising messages on television and radio, on billboards, at sporting events, and on the Internet. One would think they get a break from all those commercials when they go to school, but perhaps not.

Welcome to Couldbeyour School. As the bus picks you up, you notice the ad for Sprite soda emblazoned on the side. When you get to school, you are given free book covers for your texts. Great! Hey, what's this? Each one has an advertisement on it. Your teacher flips on Channel One for the daily news. Between news reports are ads for Reebok sneakers, Mountain Dew soda, and other products. Enough news—time for science. It's a unit on nuclear energy.

The packet bears the logo of a utility company. Isn't that the company that runs the nearby nuclear power plant? As you change classes, you notice the posters in the hallway advertising some food and soda products. Outside the window, you spot the school's new scoreboard on the football field. Say, isn't that a Pepsi logo?[22] While this example is extreme, each of these forms of advertising has taken place in American schools.

Other advertising comes in the form of "educational" films such as *Sugar—The Necessary Ingredient*, *The Great American Chocolate Story*, and *Peanut News and Views*. Free materials, particularly for today's underfunded school systems, can be irresistible. But Alex Molnar, a professor of education at the University of Wisconsin in Milwaukee, says that the schools are selling students to people who want to use them. "As soon as you have a special interest producing materials for purposes related to a particular agenda, you undermine the legitimacy of that school curriculum," says Molnar.[23]

Some of the materials are useful and well-designed, and they blend well into the school's curricula. Others are blatant propaganda, self-serving, and useless. "It's not that all the information is false," says Charlotte Baecher, director of education services at Consumers Union. "But many state opinions as fact. When we were evaluating those curriculums we had Consumers Union's technical staff at our disposal. The kids and teachers don't."[24]

Other advertisers use schools as sales representatives. Administrators eager to boost budgets encourage kids to collect labels and box tops from canned goods, cereals, and other consumer products. Fast-food restaurants offer special school nights, during which a small portion of the profits are given to the school. It is obvious how the companies benefit: More people buy their products, they gain goodwill, and they receive publicity—all at very little cost to them. What is less clear is how the kids—who are being encouraged to eat even more salty, fatty, sugary, processed foods—are benefiting.

One way that advertisers reach children at school is through Channel One, a daily TV news program interspersed with advertisements that is provided to middle schools and high schools for free. The company says that it reaches 40 percent of all middle and high school students in the United States.[25] Although Channel One markets itself as a valuable news resource for schools, critics say it is simply an advertising delivery system. New York State banned it after determining that it held little educational value.[26]

As more and more schools go on-line, children's exposure to advertising will continue to grow. The number of children with classroom access to the Internet is expected to go from 1.5 million in 1996 to more than 20 million by 2002.[27]

7

Impact on Kids

Advertising has a thousand principles, one purpose, and no morals.

—Mr. Dooley, a fictional character created by humorist Finley Peter Dunne, 1909

The Campaign to Woo Young Consumers

Few deny the power of advertising to influence children. A study on the persuasive power of television advertising looked at children's Christmas wish lists at the beginning and at the end of the peak toy advertising season. The children were first tested to measure their ability to

81

understand and form attitudes about ads. Initially, children with the strongest ability to distinguish advertising messages picked fewer of the TV-promoted toys than children who were more susceptible. By the end of the commercial period, however, massive advertising campaigns were able to overcome the defenses of even the children with the strongest resistance to commercial appeals.[1]

One reason for advertising's power is its ability to blend into programming. Most children younger than age six do not understand that the purpose of an advertisement is to sell a product.[2] Nicholas Rouillard, a nine-year-old interviewed for an article in *Business Week*, defined the difference between an ad and a TV program by saying: "Commercials are shorter. A commercial is one minute long, but a cartoon can last up to two hours."[3]

It *has* become confusing. Characters from TV shows and films are now printed on everything from food packages to bedsheets. They become toys, books, games, and computer programs. The companies that make and market spin-off products often get into the action very early in the game. The company that helped design the car used in a Warner Brothers' *Batman* movie wasn't Ford or Chevrolet, it was Hasbro, a toy manufacturer.[4]

Almost everything kids read, see, hear, or experience has a sales message somewhere in it. Some say that this has made kids more aware of commercialism and more selective in their choices. Others say that kids become numbed by the barrage and ignore the messages. But critics worry that the overwhelming amount of advertising has made kids greedy, selfish, and materialistic.

Hitting the Insecurity Hot Button

Ads targeted at teenagers often cater to the teen's desire for independence, sophistication, social success, masculinity or femininity, and good looks. But they imply that meeting those needs requires certain products and brand names. They play on teenagers' concerns about what's cool and imply that without the product, the teenager will never be popular.

The creation of an image for the brand is particularly important for "badge" products, those that teens use to send signals to other teenagers about who they

Some advertisements warn people about the dangers of smoking, drinking, and taking illegal drugs. This ad is a parody of cigarette billboards that show cowboys enjoying a smoke. In this case, one of the men tells the other that he has a respiratory illness caused by years of smoking.

are. With badge products such as athletic shoes, jeans, and soft drinks, brand image is everything.

Is using insecurity as a marketing tool fair? Teenagers are already so consumed with fitting in that problems from drug use to suicide have been linked to severe insecurity. Is it wise to reinforce self-doubt in such a vulnerable audience?

Insecurity is such a primary motivator among teenagers that some experts feel it should be used in antidrug and antismoking advertising. Telling kids something is for adults, that it's dangerous and perhaps even deadly, virtually guarantees that it will seem (you guessed it) *more* appealing to teenagers. Instead of using a "drugs = death" approach to discourage teen drug use, says Bob Garfield in *Advertising Age*, "drugs = ugly" would be much more terrifying. He points to a new series of ads featuring heroin addicts such as Lenny, who shows off pus-filled needle tracks, and a model who pulls out her false teeth to demonstrate heroin's ravages.[5] Columnist Sandy McIntosh has suggested that if brand names such as Marlboro, Virginia Slims, and Camel were changed to names like Loser, Pimples, and Immature few teenagers would find them so appealing.[6]

Impact on Children's Health

One of the biggest concerns regarding advertising to children is its effects on their health—mental as well as physical. The world depicted in commercials is one of people striving to be thinner, better looking, and richer. Honesty doesn't pay, conformity rules, and thinking of others is for wimps. The value system is one of greed, jealousy, and concern only for what other people think.

Above all, advertising teaches a superficial, live-for-the-moment philosophy that can influence already rebellious teenagers. As Mary Pipher, a clinical psychologist who wrote the book *Reviving Ophelia: Saving the Selves of Adolescent Girls*, puts it, "We are taught to go for it. We're encouraged that if it feels right, it is right."[7] Pipher says that the idea that life's difficulties should be remedied by buying unnecessary products is a dangerous one. The need for immediate gratification can lead to using drugs, comforting oneself with food, or having irresponsible sex.

Critics wonder whether a preoccupation with possessions encourages children to shoplift, steal from other kids, and lie. Without commercials emphasizing the critical need for the "right" clothing, would there be cases of kids killing kids for a particular brand of jacket or shoes?

Commercials have also been criticized for promoting sexuality at an early age. Ads for young children show them in provocative poses, wearing makeup, and imitating adult behavior. Some critics blame the media, including advertising, for rushing children into becoming adults. They say this practice may encourage teens to prematurely enter into sexual relationships.

Girls feel particular pressure to be thin and pretty. "Get a Thinner, Firmer, Cuter Body!" "How I Lost 37 Pounds and Had the Best Summer of My Life!" scream the ads. Messages like these target teenage girls who are insecure about themselves. "This summer, you can either have a lot of fun at the pool in your cute new bikini. Or, you can wear a one-piece swimsuit that's just like your grandma's," warns one ad. "Order Now . . . and Change Your Life *Forever*!" promises another.

Many critics feel that the use of fashion models who are unrealistically thin, combined with advertisements that make thinness seem all-important, contributes to the incidence of eating disorders among young women.

Advertising may also have contributed to the change in the way teenagers (particularly girls) see themselves. In 1892 an American teenager wrote in her diary, "Resolved, not to talk about myself or feelings. To work seriously. To be dignified. Interest myself more in others." Nearly one hundred years later a modern teenager described her own plans for self-improvement: "I will lose weight. Get new lenses, already got new haircut, good makeup, new clothes and accessories." In the book *The Body Project*, author Joan Jacobs Brumberg described how teenage girls' thinking about themselves has changed since the advent of such products as Clearasil and training bras.[8] The increasing focus on superficial appearance has resulted in girls' obsessions with their bodies and a drop in self-esteem, according to Brumberg. These factors can contribute to eating disorders such as anorexia.

Young children's health may suffer as well. Nine of ten food ads on Saturday morning television are for sugary cereals and candy bars, salty canned foods, fatty fast foods, and other junk food.[9] Manufacturers of these products know that kids like them and will ask for them (and often get them) over the objections of parents who know they aren't healthy.

Alcohol, Tobacco, and Firearm Advertising to Children

One of the biggest concerns with alcohol advertising is its role in promoting underage drinking. Although alcohol marketers stress that they would never purposely target underage consumers, the products often seem specially designed to appeal to young, inexperienced drinkers.

It is difficult to imagine a mature drinker being interested in a liqueur like Tattoo, for example. The sixty-proof "shooter" comes in licorice, berry, and lemon flavors and contains a substance that temporarily dyes the drinkers' tongues red, blue, or yellow.[10]

Philip Van Munching, a former beer advertiser and son of a beer importer, criticizes products such as a frozen malt liquor (sort of a beer-sicle) called St. Ides Special Blend Freeze and Squeeze, test-marketed in inner-city stores by the McKenzie River Corporation. (The company halted the test-marketing following public complaints.)[11]

Van Munching says that beer, in particular, has been associated not only with mindless partying but also with underage mindless partying. A heavy beer drinker in his twenties is not terribly different in his behavior and outlook from a fourteen year old, says

Van Munching, so the advertising portrays the babes-and-beer attitude to which some teenage males also respond.[12]

Although the industry denies it targets young people, the evidence sometimes shows otherwise. An *Advertising Age* study of beer advertising on MTV during the week of September 1–7, 1996, found beer ads aired during time periods in which over half the audience was under the legal drinking age.[13]

Concerns continue that tobacco advertising messages influence children, even though modern promotions are much more subtle than this early ad.

Cigarette advertising messages also reach children. A survey conducted by James Sargent, a cancer researcher and pediatrician, found that children who own cigarette promotional items such as imprinted hats, backpacks, and T-shirts are far more likely to smoke. The survey found that, in a single day, 40 percent of the children surveyed had seen at least one of the promotional items. "We found that, in effect, children are being used to market cigarettes to their peers," said Sargent.[14]

Another industry group that has come under fire is the National Rifle Association (NRA). The group uses Eddie Eagle, a cartoon character, to teach children to handle guns safely. In November 1997 the Violence Policy Center (VPC), a nonprofit group that studies gun violence, issued a 144-page analysis that said the NRA is using the character to put a friendly face on a hazardous product that cannot legally be sold to children. The VPC study suggested that the NRA is trying to create a new generation of gun owners, using the same techniques the tobacco industry has used to hook children on cigarettes. Marion Hammer, president of the NRA, said that the firearms industry is "like any other industry. If you rely on today's customers to carry you forever, then you're going to be out of business soon." But, according to Hammer, "Eddie Eagle has nothing to do with the marketing of guns."[15]

8

Advertising in Sheep's Clothing

There is no hour of waking life in which we are not besought, incited, or commanded to buy something of somebody.

—Journalist Samuel Hopkins Adams, 1909

Athletes as Walking Billboards

In the movie *Peggy Sue Got Married*, Peggy Sue goes back in time to her high school days of 1960. She tells Richard, a profit-minded student who is eager to know what the future holds, "I'll tell you where there's a real fortune to be made—running shoes." Richard responds incredulously,

"You've got to be kidding me. You're talking about exercise stuff, like *gym* stuff?"

Salomon Brothers, a financial services company, predicts that by the year 2000 the market for athletic footwear—gym shoes—will be $8.5 billion.[1] In part, athletic shoes have become a huge market because young people idolize sports stars, and sports stars wear expensive name-brand athletic shoes. Why? Because they are paid to. Paid a lot. Michael Jordan, at the top of the endorsement mountain, gets $40 million a year ($10 million more than he gets for playing basketball) for lending his name to a variety of products. And that was *before* he started raking in his 10 percent of the proceeds from the movie *Space Jam* (which featured numerous plugs for those same athletic shoes).[2]

What started as happy accidents are now carefully controlled marketing programs. In 1960 a skier who used Rossignol skis won the gold medal in the Olympics. The Rossignol Ski Company was quickly buried in an

Nike has built such a strong brand identity that a photograph of a shoe bearing the familiar "swoosh" is all that is needed to advertise the product.

avalanche of orders. Rossignol made sure that their luck would continue. By 1984 the company was paying more than two hundred champion skiers from eighteen countries to use only Rossignol equipment.[3]

Athletes (and other celebrities) help companies create a symbolic association for their product. Such symbols help consumers define themselves by which products they choose. Steve Barnett, a corporate anthropologist (someone who studies the culture of companies), says that the hunt for symbols is increasing because "more and more products are essentially equivalent." "Look at Nike and Reebok," says Barnett. "They're entirely focused on creating strong symbols, in part using athletes, in part using other advertising techniques. In fact, the shoes are exactly the same."[4]

In 1990, Buddy Ryan, head coach of the Philadelphia Eagles football team, began wearing a black cap with a green bill and an eagle logo. Within the first few weeks, sharp-eyed fans bought two thousand of the seventeen dollar hats. Ryan had been paid a reported twenty-five thousand dollars to wear the cap at games and practices.[5] Disney pays athletes to make endorsements moments after a win. A narrator asks the athletes where they are going now, to which they respond, "I'm going to Disneyland!"

Event Sponsorship

It may seem generous for companies to help fund popular events such as tennis or golf tournaments, races, or festivals. Although the companies receive tremendous goodwill from such sponsorships, the practice is actually an advertising tool. Sponsorships are selected for the audiences they deliver and the environment in which their product is placed. For example, a cigarette company that wants to promote a women's brand of cigarettes, Virginia Slims, sponsors a women's tennis tournament. Their product is seen by millions of potential customers in a setting of fitness, excitement, and female empowerment— exactly the way the makers of Virginia Slims cigarettes want the product to be perceived. Sponsors of events are often companies with "difficult" products or those with image problems to overcome: cigarette makers, oil companies, banks, chemical manufacturers, and so forth. Even if people come away feeling "they're not so bad," the company has come out ahead.

Corporate sponsorship is also used to fill the ever-widening gap between what the public will fund through taxes and what it wants. The Smithsonian's exotic bug exhibit is named the "O. Orkin Insect Zoo" and is sponsored by the Orkin Pest Control company. Could this be why there is a prominently displayed Orkin logo but no mention of the harmful effects of pesticides?[6]

Product Placements

When ET, the charming alien in the movie *ET: The Extraterrestrial*, followed the trail of Reese's Pieces, it was the product's manufacturer, Hershey Chocolate, that found treasure—a sales increase reported to be 85 percent.[7] Although the company didn't pay to

Although it wasn't a paid placement, the important role Reese's Pieces played in the film ET *resulted in huge sales increases.*

have their product placed in the film, they spent $1 million to promote the tie-in.[8]

Product placement began as an organized business in the late 1970s. By the mid-1980s there were about thirty companies whose sole purpose was to place products in films and television programs.

Writers and directors have always used props to add authenticity to a scene—a bounty hunter might chug a beer while a society matron would sip expensive champagne. Now, companies pay a fee to have the moviemakers use their brand-name product in the scene.

In the 1993 thriller *Demolition Man*, Taco Bell was depicted as the only fast-food company to survive the "franchise wars" of the twentieth century. The movie's producers had the script rewritten to specify Taco Bell, and in exchange, Taco Bell promoted the film in all its restaurants.[9]

Product placements have become more and more obvious in recent years. Bags of branded snack foods are consumed in a distracting manner, products loom in the foregrounds of scenes in which they serve no purpose, and actual ads (billboards, signs, etc.) appear as backdrops. According to court records, Reebok International said they provided $1.5 million worth of shoes, cash, and clothing, as well as football training, for the actors in the film *Jerry Maguire*. In exchange, they expected a phony Reebok ad to be run over the credits at the end of the movie. The commercial never appeared and Reebok sued. The case was later settled.[10]

The appearance of a product in a film is only part of the story. Advertisers also strike deals to promote connections between their product and the movie. The award for ultimate achievement in this area must go to *Tomorrow Never Dies*, a James Bond movie that was promoted by five major advertisers in a $98 million cross-promotional deal. TV viewers saw James Bond (actor Pierce Brosnan) using a Visa Check Card, driving a BMW, chatting on an Ericsson cell phone, and leaping off a roof onto a Heineken beer truck in a blitz of ads tied to the film's release. *Newsweek* called the movie an "ad extravaganza" in an article titled "Licensed To Shill."[11]

Seeing a product used in a realistic way by characters the viewer admires, in a story in which the viewer is emotionally involved, can leave a powerful impression. As Peter Thomas, marketing manager for Perrier in the United Kingdom said: "This sort of exposure is very important to us because it's all part of getting Perrier into the fabric of society. It's a very subtle way of selling."[12]

Television has not been left behind. For years, game shows consisted of little more than excuses for promoting products (the prizes). *The Price Is Right* show alone promoted fifty products per show. Now, there are whole channels devoted to advertising. The most familiar of these is MTV, which consists almost exclusively of music videos (advertisements for recordings) interrupted by advertisements. Other channels are devoted to "home shopping," in which products are sold over the air.

Even music videos have become placement vehicles. When country singer Alan Jackson was shown at the wheel of a Big Foot Ford F-150 pickup truck— along with five Ford Nascar drivers and assorted other Ford vehicles—in the video for his single "Who's Cheatin' Who," it wasn't just chance, it was a product placement. Ford has a multi-million-dollar deal with the singer to promote its products.[13]

As the public becomes more aware of product placement, will this form of advertising still work or will people simply feel manipulated? Perhaps one day we'll see a return to the sly honesty of Alfred Hitchcock, who introduced commercials during his 1950s television shows with such conspicuous lead-ins as "And now as a service to you television addicts who are trying to give it up, here, before I return, is something that will certainly do the trick," and (during a shipboard story) "I feel I must move to the rail; we are about to have one of our commercials."[14]

Infomercials—Commercials in Disguise

You're flipping through the TV channels before heading off to class. There is *Good Morning America*, *The Today Show*, and something called *Morning Edition*. It looks similar—the hosts sit on comfortable chairs around a coffee table and greet guests. But there is a major difference. This morning the topic is watches, and each one is for sale. The program is a medium for advertising and selling products. There is no other content.

In the 1960s long commercials were banned when the FCC restricted advertising time on television. But the rules were relaxed in 1984 under President Ronald Reagan's deregulation effort. The *infomercial*, or informative commercial, was born. As the number of cable stations grew, the number of infomercials exploded. Ads lasting thirty minutes (instead of the normal thirty *seconds*) grew quickly into a $450-million-a-year business and may now be over $1 billion.[15]

Now, there are huge blocks of time on some cable stations devoted to "paid programming." The shows have the look, feel, and length of regular television programs. They may even be interrupted by "commercials." But the programs themselves—the entire thirty minutes (or more)—have been purchased as advertising time. The product may be discussed as a "breakthrough" by experts on what seems like a talk show or investigative news program. Nevertheless, the program is simply a sophisticated advertisement.

The hosts and experts gush enthusiasm for the

products they show (it's what they're paid to do). They create a sense of urgency, encouraging the audience to act quickly, to get in on the deal, not to miss out. This appeal to impulsiveness, combined with an aggressive sales approach and an audience heavily weighted with homebound, elderly, and bored viewers, virtually guarantees huge sales.

Product-oriented shows are not the only programs clamoring for audience dollars. Many religious programs are also just thinly veiled appeals for money. Viewers are urged not to "miss God's call," asked to become "partners," invited to join a club, or encouraged to buy products such as prayer cloths. Program hosts may promise prayers in exchange for donations or suggest that donors will be rewarded with riches through some sort of divine intervention. Proof may be offered in the form of *testimonials*, stories from donors who claim to have won lotteries or received unexpected rewards after making donations. Unfortunately, the religious trappings imposed on these promotions often appeal to the elderly, ill, or downtrodden—those who may be least able to afford to give their money away.

Public Television

Advertisers have long pushed to open the Public Broadcasting System (PBS) to traditional advertising. Initially designed as an alternative to commercial television, PBS is funded by government funds and donations. However, corporate donations led to corporate underwriting, which allowed sponsors to have a brief message before or after the program.

In some cases today, it is difficult to tell PBS sponsorship messages from the ads that appear on commercial stations. And while viewers may see corporate donations to public broadcasting as generous charitable contributions, they are simply another form of advertising.

PBS watchers tend to have higher education and income levels than most other commercial television viewers. General Motors Corporation (GM) recognized those characteristics as the same as those of most new-car and truck buyers. "There may be more of an opportunity to hit a home run on PBS than there is on other channels," said Phil Guarascio, GM's general manager of marketing and advertising, of the company's $15 to $20 million sponsorship of Ken Burns's productions. Supporting the programs "might not be very different from an N.F.L. licensing agreement," said Guarascio.[16]

While some critics worry about the growing involvement of commercial interests in public television, increasing cuts in funding combined with rising production costs have made corporate funding a necessity.

9

Brave New World

The art of advertising is now so near to perfection that it is not easy to propose any improvement.

—Samuel Johnson, 1761

They Know Where You Live

Advertisers can buy the names and addresses of dentists who own airplanes, people who raise snakes, men who are bald, and women living in Toledo who vote Republican. They know who is likely to buy a Chevrolet and who wouldn't be caught dead in platform shoes. How do they know? We tell them.

Virtually every piece of paper (or

on-line computer form) you fill out makes its way into the hands of companies wanting to sell you something. Even change-of-address coupons sent to the U.S. Postal Service are used to send you packets of coupons, ads, and free samples. Credit reporting companies sell lists of people in specific financial categories. If you buy from telephone solicitors, fill out product registrations, or subscribe to magazines, your actions are recorded and then your name and address are placed on lists that are bought and sold without your knowledge. Send in a warranty card for a computer product and you'll start receiving catalogs for software. Make a purchase from a catalog and you better get a bigger mailbox for all the additional catalogs you'll be receiving.

The availability of massive amounts of personal information on computers has made "knowing your audience" a reality for advertisers. Virtually every major event and most minor ones in your life are recorded, compiled, and, in many cases, sold for advertising purposes.

Timing advertising pitches with personal milestones is a technique called *synchographics*. Manufacturers of baby products buy lists of women who have just given birth. Furniture companies buy lists of people who have just moved. Companies that market breast-milk substitutes (formula) time their mailings to arrive during the period when most new mothers experience difficulty breast-feeding.[1] Lists of kids approaching driving age, high school students, and teens likely to go to college are also popular with advertisers. Is this smart marketing or exploitation?

Marketers buy lists of kids as well. *Sesame Street* magazine rents its subscriber list. Hasbro Toys sold the names of people who sent in proof of purchase labels to get a rebate on My Little Pony games and other products. Marketers can even buy a list of the kids who mailed in a request for a live tadpole for their Grow A Frog kit.[2]

They Know Who You Are

The personal information that advertisers can access is staggering. Even data such as income and credit information can often be accessed, as can some police and legal records. (If anyone in your family has an accident or injury, watch your mailbox for the letters from lawyers.) Telephone companies have sold information about customers' travel habits (based on their telephone calling-card patterns). State motor vehicle departments provide car registration information to marketers on easy-to-use computer tapes. The Publishers Clearing House Sweepstakes uses contest entries not only to build a database but to spot gullible consumers ("opportunity seekers") who might be receptive to other offers.[3]

Critics are concerned about the right to privacy. "With privacy issues, victims are not obvious," says Janlori Goldman, an attorney with the American Civil Liberties Union. "Harm is not identifiable. There's no blood, there's no body, no broken bones." Yet she feels harm is done. "It affects the choices you make, it affects the way you live, it affects your sense of being an individual, of being autonomous, of being able to live in the world without always being watched, without always being monitored."[4]

One way to identify potential customers is to identify the people most likely to buy a product based on their income, education, or other characteristics. In the 1940s W. Lloyd Warner developed a way to group consumers by class. He used occupation, source of income, education, family background, and area of residence to group people into identifiable categories such as "locally prominent families," "merchants," "executive elite," "unskilled," and "unassimilated ethnic groups."[5] Although these were general categories that were helpful for developing advertising campaigns, they did not identify specific individuals within the categories that could be approached one-on-one.

More Sophisticated Groupings

In the 1970s and 1980s psychological groupings became popular. Marketers appealed to specific groups such as the infamous yuppies (young, upwardly mobile professionals).

One of the best-known classification systems was VALS (Values and Lifestyles), which divided Americans into nine lifestyle groups, from "survivors," who are struggling to exist, to "integrated," who have it all together. Timex Corporation used VALS in marketing a new line of home health care products in the 1980s. Within months the products had become the biggest sellers in the marketplace.

Although some professionals scoffed at VALS and called it a hoax, many advertisers swore by it.[6]

Marketers now have even more sophisticated classification systems (including an updated VALS system) for identifying and profiling prospective customers. One such system, called PRIZM (Potential Rating Index for Zip Markets), is offered by Claritas, Inc. It is based on the "birds of a feather flock together" idea—people tend to seek out neighborhoods where people like themselves live.

Claritas uses census data, zip code information, and actual consumer buying records to develop "lifestyle clusters" based on income, education, mobility, ethnicity, housing density, home value, and other factors. The clusters have names that reflect the kinds of lifestyles such behaviors indicate. For example, "Shotguns and Pickups" are white, have a high school or grade school education, smoke pipe tobacco, drink Canadian whisky, listen to country music, and read hunting magazines; whereas "Executive Suites" are white or Asian, have a college education, play racquetball, own a camcorder, listen to jazz, and use financial planning services. There are over sixty such groupings, ranging from "Blue Blood Estates" to "Hard Scrabble."[7]

Lifestyle classification systems allow advertisers to focus their advertising in a tightly targeted way. And unlike earlier lifestyle classification systems, the new methods supply more than just marketing categories, they supply individual names and addresses.

This type of targeting system, called *geodemographics*, combines geographic information (where one lives) with demographic data (information about people) to create a powerful predictor of consumer buying behavior. Companies can analyze their existing customers to see which cluster groups tend to be their biggest buyers. Then they can purchase lists of other people in that cluster and target them with mailings.[8]

Is this Big Brother peeking in your windows or simply a better way to get you the information you need to make buying decisions? Is this marketing efficiency or stereotyping? Cost effectiveness or demeaning insult? In theory at least, geodemographic marketing should make sure old Aunt Prudence doesn't get mailings from tattoo parlors and assure that teenaged Heather isn't bombarded with discounts on false teeth adhesives. We all want to be known for who we are, right?

New Technology

Scanning technology (the bar code system used to scan products at the supermarket) has helped advertisers become even more sophisticated. Stores can program scanners to issue coupons based on a consumer's purchases. If the shopper buys hot dogs, for example, a coupon for an advertiser's brand of mustard automatically prints out.

An intelligent supermarket cart made by VideOcart, Inc., even displays ads and coupons while the consumer is shopping. VideOcart uses sensors to display an advertising message on the computer monitor mounted on the cart as the shopper approaches the product. If the consumer wants to buy it, he or she simply presses a button to signal the store computer to deduct the coupon amount at checkout.[9]

Information Resources Inc. (IRI) has developed a way to use human guinea pigs in test-marketing programs. IRI selects a representative town. They install scanners in each store and have the area's cable television fed through their studio so they can manipulate the commercials. Consumers are invited to join the Shopper's Hotline by filling out a detailed questionnaire. Then, each time the consumers shop, their ID cards are scanned, along with their purchases. Advertisers who buy the BehaviorScan service are able to test new products, commercials, coupons, and other tactics on real live consumers.[10]

Will advertisers one day be able to monitor everyone's moves this closely? Perhaps identifiers such as Social Security numbers or fingerprints will be required for everything from voting to buying bread.

Should people care whether researchers are looking at their groceries? Suppose the researchers sold the names of people who bought reduced-fat margarine to companies selling weight-loss products. Suppose someone's purchases included condoms or home testing kits for pregnancy or AIDS. Is it right for companies to gather such personal information and then use it to sell products?

Companies say that such intelligent technology helps them improve their marketing techniques, saving everyone time and money. Products improve, they say, because feedback is immediate. Yet as Erik Larson, author of *The Naked Consumer*, points out,

Instead of refining the products they sell, they have concentrated on refining the tools of selling.[11]

A Look Toward the Future

Advertising has become an accepted part of American life. Television commercials can now win Emmy awards, an honor previously reserved for television programs of the highest caliber. Televised sports events interrupt play with "TV (advertising) time-outs." Children play with toys that are little more than three-dimensional ads for movies or television shows. Television programs are created as blocks to fit around commercials, and movie scripts are changed to accommodate paid product placements. Political campaigns find out what people want to hear and use advertising to create the candidate.

Increasingly, businesses are injecting themselves into schools, neighborhoods, entertainment, even houses of worship. Public entities struggling with the effects of tax cuts seem unable to resist the lure (or the pressure) corporate money brings. Advertising and promotion seems to be everywhere: Santa Claus has a Web page, children trick-or-treat as branded products such as M&Ms and the Pillsbury Dough Boy, bananas wear stickers promoting milk, restaurants project ads onto the sidewalks in front of their buildings, and a seemingly innocent fortune cookie was found to have the message "If you are still hungry, have another fortune cookie."

The line between culture and commercialism is becoming increasingly blurred. Advertising and entertainment have become virtually indistinguishable. People talk about a new ad with the same degree of enthusiasm that they discuss the latest episode of *Friends* or last night's basketball game.

In the future, will we live on McDonald's Lane, go to Pepsi High School, and visit the Reebok Art Gallery? Will we come to rely on businesses to fund education, arts, and entertainment, only to find that diverse, creative, and sometimes controversial projects are shelved in favor of bland, mindless, and shallow productions that make better mass-market showcases for advertising messages? Will advertisers, with access to personal information about every individual, be the Big Brother people once feared the government might become?

One of the arguments given in support of advertising is that it helps create a democratic marketplace in which everyone has access to the same products and services. But as marketers fine-tune their targeting efforts, they are able to pick and choose the potential customers they approach. Hospitals can direct mailings to residents likely to have private insurance, for example. Author Erik Larson thinks we may be replacing racial and religious discrimination with socioeconomic class discrimination through what he calls a "digital caste system."[12]

Will privacy concerns cause companies to rethink their data collection practices, or will corporate access to private information continue to grow? Some critics have pointed to past abuses to warn of the danger of today's massive databases. During World

War II the Western War Command (with the help of government census data) identified areas on the West Coast where Americans of Japanese heritage lived. This information helped them "relocate" Japanese-Americans to camps where they were held against their will for the duration of the war.[13] Today, all it takes is a phone call to obtain lists of Jewish households, people who support abortion rights, subscribers to gay publications, and thousands of other categories.

Some people feel that advertising to children should be prohibited. Children would be less materialistic and status-conscious without commercials egging them on, they say. Their diets would be better without the heavily promoted sodas, junk foods, and sugary cereals parents buy to please their children. And companies would be forced to make better quality toys rather than rely on flashy advertising.

On the other hand, if children are not exposed to advertising, how will they learn to be discriminating consumers as adults? If children are taught how to evaluate commercial content and use critical thinking skills to make their own buying decisions, they may be better prepared for the commercial world in which we live.

Conclusion

So what is advertising? Is it, as turn-of-the-century advertising executives thought, "salesmanship-on-paper?"[14] Is it, as believers in subliminal advertising thought, a form of mind control? Is it, as some parents fear, a way for businesses to go around parents to manipulate children? Or is it, as advertisers would like us to believe, an essential part of the democratic marketplace that helps consumers choose products and encourages companies to improve products? It is probably all these things. Consumers (including young people) must learn to use their critical thinking skills to evaluate advertising messages and determine which ones, if any, to believe.

Tips for Critically Evaluating Advertising

1. Remember that the primary purpose of an advertisement is to make you want to buy something.

2. Ask yourself whether the product will actually provide the benefits shown in the advertisement especially if the benefits are social or psychological (happiness, popularity, success, etc.).

3. Consider that some of the components shown in the ad may not be included, that the product may require special skills or practice to use, and that it may have to be assembled.

4. Remember that the product is being shown not only under optimum conditions, but in some cases (through special effects) better than optimum conditions.

5. Realize that sports figures, movie and TV stars, singers, and even "experts" who endorse products in commercials are simply

being paid to read carefully constructed scripts.

6. Be aware that most recognizable brands of food, clothing, cars, beverages, or other products shown in movies or on television have been placed there intentionally for a fee by an advertiser.

7. Keep in mind that people appearing in advertisements are almost always professional actors or models playing a role. Even people who look like "regular" people are generally professional actors.

8. Understand that models (male and female) have had their hair, nails, and makeup done by professionals, are photographed using flattering techniques, and spend lots of time and money creating the best possible body. The products they model will probably not look the same on you (no offense).

9. Realize that the primary goal of some full-length television shows, "informational" programs, and films is to sell products.

10. Be on alert when ads flatter you, tell you how cool you are, or admire you for being a rebel—they are after your wallet.

11. Watch out for "weasel" words like *helps*, *often*, *may*, and *virtually*. These qualifiers water down claims enough to make them legal (and "virtually" meaningless).

12. Remember that if something seems too good to be true, it probably is.

Chapter Notes

Chapter 1. Creating Want

1. David Leonhardt and Kathleen Kerwin, "Hey Kid, Buy This!" *Business Week*, June 30, 1997, pp. 62–67.

2. Leslie Savan, *The Sponsored Life: Ads, TV, and American Culture* (Philadelphia: Temple University Press, 1994), p. 1.

3. Susan Headden, "The Junk Mail Deluge," *U.S. News & World Report*, December 8, 1997, p. 40.

4. Robert J. Coen, "Ad Revenue Growth Hits 7% in 1997 to Surpass Forecasts," *Advertising Age*, May 18, 1998, p. 50.

5. Michael Schudson, *Advertising, The Uneasy Persuasion: Its Dubious Impact on American Society* (New York: BasicBooks, 1984), pp. 169–171.

6. Stephen Fox, *The Mirror Makers: A History of American Advertising and Its Creators* (New York: William Morrow, 1984), p. 16.

7. Ibid., p. 66.

8. Ann E. Weiss, *The School on Madison Avenue: Advertising and What It Teaches* (New York: E. P. Dutton, 1980), p. 18.

9. Fox, p. 67.

10. Erik Larson, *The Naked Consumer: How Our Private Lives Become Public Commodities* (New York: Henry Holt, 1992), p. 21.

11. Ibid.

12. Ibid., pp. 21–22.

13. Eric Clark, *The Want Makers: The World of Advertising* (New York: Viking, 1988), p. 324.

14. Erik Barnouw, *The Sponsor: Notes on a Modern Potentate* (New York: Oxford University Press, 1978), p. 46.

15. Fox, p. 172.

16. Ibid., p. 212.

17. Vance Packard, *The Hidden Persuaders* (New York: David McKay, 1957), p. 3.

18. James B. Twitchell, *Adcult USA: The Triumph of Advertising in American Culture* (New York: Columbia University Press, 1996), pp. 111–114.

19. Fox, p. 318.

Chapter 2. The Hows and Whys of Advertising

1. Alex Kuczynski, "Hold Me! Squeeze Me! Buy a 6-Pack!" *The New York Times*, November 16, 1997, section 9, p. 4.

2. Nike financial statement, May 31, 1998, <http://www.nikebiz.com/invest_m.html> (July 7, 1998).

3. Eric Clark, *The Want Makers: The World of Advertising* (New York: Viking, 1988), p. 25

4. Andrea Codrington, "Public Eye," *The New York Times*, January 29, 1998, p. F2.

5. Stephen Fox, *The Mirror Makers: A History of American Advertising and Its Creators* (New York: William Morrow, 1984), pp. 222–223.

6. Kuczynski, p. 4.

7. Kenneth Wylie, "100 Leading Research Companies," *Advertising Age*, May 25, 1998, p. s1.

8. Erik Larson, *The Naked Consumer: How Our Private Lives Become Public Commodities* (New York: Henry Holt, 1992), p. 9.

9. Leslie Kaufman, "Enough Talk," *Newsweek*, August 18, 1997, p. 49.

10. Selina S. Guber and Jon Berry, *Marketing to and Through Kids* (New York: McGraw-Hill, 1993), p. 138.

11. Fox, pp. 298–299.

12. Leslie Savan, *The Sponsored Life: Ads, TV, and American Culture* (Philadelphia: Temple University Press, 1994), pp. 117–119.

13. Ibid., p. 134.

14. Scott Shane, "Direct Mail Aims at Heart," *Baltimore Sun*, December 21, 1997, p. 1A.

15. Ibid., p. 6A.

16. Ibid.

17. Fox, p. 65.

18. Ibid., p. 68.

19. Ibid., p. 168.

20. Ibid., p. 319.

21. Ibid., pp. 319–320.

Chapter 3. Advertising's Role in American Culture

1. Samm Sinclair Baker, *The Permissible Lie: The Inside Truth About Advertising* (New York: World, 1968), pp. 180–181.

2. Ibid., p. 190.

3. Eric Clark, *The Want Makers: The World of Advertising* (New York: Viking, 1988), p. 324.

4. "Advertising in Disguise," *Consumer Reports*, March 1986, pp. 179–181.

5. Clark, p. 347.

6. Kenneth E. Warner, Linda M. Goldenhar, and Catherine G. McLaughlin, "Cigarette Advertising and Magazine Coverage of the Hazards of Smoking: A Statistical Analysis," *The New England Journal of Medicine,* January 30, 1992, vol. 326, pp. 305–309.

7. Amanda Amos, Bobbie Jacobson, and Patti White, "Cigarette Advertising Policy and Coverage of Smoking and Health in British Women's Magazines," *The Lancet*, January 12, 1991, vol. 337, pp. 93–95.

8. Robin Morgan, personal communication with author, August 7, 1992.

9. Chuck Ross, "New TV Show Producer Offers Advertiser Input," *Advertising Age*, January 27, 1997, p. 4.

10. Erik Larson, *The Naked Consumer: How Our Private Lives Become Public Commodities* (New York: Henry Holt, 1992), p. 20.

11. Michael Schudson, *Advertising, The Uneasy Persuasion: Its Dubious Impact on American Society* (New York: BasicBooks, 1984), pp. 181–182.

12. Peter K. Francese, "Big Spenders," *American Demographics*, August 1997, pp. 51–57.

13. Ira Teinowitz, "House Softens Tobacco-Curbs Plan," *Advertising Age*, June 29, 1998, p. 52.

14. Edmund L. Andrews, "European Officials Agree to Ban on Most Cigarette Ads by 2006," *The New York Times*, December 5, 1997, p. A1.

15. Steve Rhodes and Leslie Kaufman, "Winston's Naked Appeal," *Newsweek*, September 8, 1997, pp. 60, 62.

16. Clark, p. 285.

17. Ibid., p. 293.

18. Ibid., p. 305.

19. Stephen Ansolabehere and Shanto Iyengar, *Going Negative: How Attack Ads Shrink and Polarize the Electorate* (New York: Free Press, 1996), p. 108.

20. Ibid., p. 149.

Chapter 4. Getting Attention at Any Cost

1. Eric Clark, *The Want Makers: The World of Advertising* (New York: Viking, 1988), p. 328.

2. Paul D. Colford, "Neighborly Advice," *Newsday*, October 1, 1997, p. C4.

3. Nzong Xiong, "Web Advertising Beyond Banners," *The New York Times*, July 28, 1997, p. D5.

4. Rikki McGinty, "Marketers See Web Games as Perfect Fit for Their Ads," *Advertising Age*, March 3, 1997, p. 26.

5. Patricia Riedman, "Geotargeting Picks Up Speed in Web Marketing Mix," *Advertising Age*, June 2, 1997, p. s18.

6. Ann Marie Kerwin, "'NY Times' Web Site Lets Advertisers Get Personal," *Advertising Age*, July 14, 1997, p. 35.

7. Noah Shachtman, "Services Vie to Handle Direct E-Mail Pitches," *Advertising Age*, June 29, 1998, p. 38.

8. Unidentified advertiser, personal communication to author, August 29, 1997.

9. Peter H. Lewis, "Many Users of Commercial On-line Services Are Getting a Steady Diet of 'Spam,'" *The New York Times*, October 20, 1997, p. D4.

10. Center for Media Education, "ABSOLUTe Web: Tobacco and Alcohol Industries Launch into Cyberspace," *InfoActive Kids*, Winter 1997, <http://tap.epn.org/cme/infoactive/w97.html> (September 11, 1997), p. 15.

11. Leslie Savan, *The Sponsored Life: Ads, TV, and American Culture* (Philadelphia: Temple University Press, 1994), pp. 169–170.

12. Michael Schudson, *Advertising, The Uneasy Persuasion: Its Dubious Impact on American Society* (New York: BasicBooks, 1984), pp. 122–125.

13. Samm Sinclair Baker, *The Permissible Lie: The Inside Truth About Advertising* (New York: World, 1968), p. 20.

14. Stephen Fox, *The Mirror Makers: A History of American Advertising and Its Creators* (New York: William Morrow, 1984), p. 319.

15. Baker, p. 16.

16. Ibid., p. 17.

Chapter 5. New and Improved Ways to Make You Buy

1. Stephen Fox, *The Mirror Makers: A History of American Advertising and Its Creators* (New York: William Morrow, 1984), pp. 324–325.

2. Helen Katz, *The Media Handbook* (Lincolnwood, Ill.: NTC Business Books, 1995), p. 13.

3. Fox, p. 325.

4. Samm Sinclair Baker, *The Permissible Lie: The Inside Truth About Advertising* (New York: World, 1968), pp. 23–24.

5. Eric Clark, *The Want Makers: The World of Advertising* (New York: Viking, 1988), p. 23.

6. Leslie Savan, *The Sponsored Life: Ads, TV, and American Culture* (Philadelphia: Temple University Press, 1994), p. 163.

7. Michael Schudson, *Advertising, The Uneasy Persuasion: Its Dubious Impact on American Society* (New York: BasicBooks, 1984), p. 174.

8. Clark, p. 183.

9. Fox, p. 320.

10. Dolores Kong, "Words from on High to Push Health in Hub," *Boston Globe*, September 30, 1992, pp. 27, 30.

11. David Satcher, interviewed by Alex Chadwick, "Minority Smoking Up," *Morning Edition, National Public Radio*, April 28, 1998.

12. Philip Van Munching, "Next: Beer on a Stick," *The New York Times*, July 26, 1997, p. 21.

13. Barry Meier, "Data on Tobacco Show a Strategy Aimed at Blacks," *The New York Times*, February 6, 1998, pp. A1, A18.

14. Michael Wilke, " 'Ellen' Offered Buying Breakthrough," *Advertising Age*, August 4, 1997, p. 11.

15. Michael Wilke, "FDA Ruling on DTC Drug Ads on TV," *Advertising Age*, June 29, 1998, p. 3.

16. Mark Landler, "Now, Worse than Ever! Cynicism in Advertising!" *The New York Times*, August 17, 1997, pp. 1E, 6E.

17. Jib Fowles, *Advertising and Popular Culture* (Thousand Oaks, Calif.: Sage Publications, 1996), pp. 179–180.

18. Peter Zollo, *Wise Up to Teens: Insights into Marketing and Advertising to Teenagers* (Ithaca, N.Y.: New Strategist Publications, 1995), pp. 43, 116, 117, 265.

19. Savan, p. 9.

Chapter 6. Targeting Kids

1. David Leonhardt and Kathleen Kerwin, "Hey Kid, Buy This!" *Business Week*, June 30, 1997, p. 62.

2. Center for Media Education, "'And Now a Web from Our Sponsor': How Online Advertisers Are Cashing in on Children," *Infoactive Kids*, Winter 1996, <http://tap.epn.org/cme/infoactive/22/22nweb.html> (September 11, 1997), p. 3.

3. Leonhardt and Kerwin, p. 66.

4. Center for Media Education, "10 Key Facts about Children and TV," n.d., <http://tap.epn.org/cme/cta/tv-facts.html> (September 11, 1997), p. 1.

5. James McNeal, "Children as Customers," *American Demographics*, September 1990, p. 39.

6. Eric Clark, *The Want Makers: The World of Advertising* (New York: Viking, 1988), p. 195.

7. Ibid., p. 196.

8. Constance L. Hays, "A Star Is Licensed," *The New York Times*, September 24, 1997, pp. D1, D4.

9. Leonhardt and Kerwin, pp. 64–65.

10. Ibid., pp. 62–63.

11. Nabisco representative, personal communication with author, July 9, 1998.

12. Larry Armstrong, "Psst! Come into My Web . . ." *Business Week*, June 30, 1997, p. 67.

13. Center for Media Education, "'And Now a Web from Our Sponsor,'" p. 2.

14. Center for Media Education, "Web of Deception: Threats to Children from Online Marketing," March 1996, <http://tap.epn.org/cme/cmwdecov.html> (September 11, 1997), p. 5.

15. Stuart Elliott, "A Clinton Adviser Argues the Economic Case for Self-Regulation of Sales Pitches in Cyberspace" *The New York Times*, November 4, 1997, p. D13.

16. Julie DeFalco, "Cyber Seducers? The Latest On-Line Outrage," n.d., <http://www.cei.org/essays/defalco1.html> (September 4, 1997).

17. Ann Marie Kerwin, "Forget Dual Audience: New Teen Magazines Go Girl Crazy," *Advertising Age*, May 19, 1997, p. 10.

18. Ibid.

19. Peter Zollo, *Wise Up to Teens: Insights into Marketing and Advertising to Teenagers* (Ithaca, N.Y.: New Strategist Publications, 1995), p. 8.

20. Ibid., p. 303.

21. Clark, pp. 185–186.

22. Pat Wechsler, "This Lesson Is Brought to You By . . .," *Business Week*, June 30, 1997, pp. 68–69.

23. Jeff Harrington, "Corporate School Programs: Educational Tools or Ads?" *Gannett News Service*, December 28, 1994.

24. Wechsler, p. 69.

25. Shelley Pasnik, "Channel One Online: Advertising Not Educating," *Center for Media Education*, n.d., <http://tap.epn.org/cme/chan1.html> (September 11, 1997), p. 1.

26. Ibid., p. 3.

27. Matthew Cravatta, "Online Adolescents," *American Demographics*, August 1997, p. 29.

Chapter 7. Impact on Kids

1. Eric Clark, *The Want Makers: The World of Advertising* (New York: Viking, 1988), p. 201.

2. Center for Media Education, "10 Key Facts about Children and TV," n.d., <http://tap.epn.org/cme/cta/tv-facts.html> (September 11, 1997), p. 1.

3. David Leonhardt and Kathleen Kerwin, "Hey Kid, Buy This!" *Business Week*, June 30, 1997, p. 66.

4. Ibid.

5. Bob Garfield, "Let Vanity Drive Ads in Anti-Drug Campaign," *Advertising Age*, March 3, 1997, p. 39.

6. Sandy McIntosh, "In Cigarettes, Names Are Addictive," *Newsday*, August 19, 1997, p. A29.

7. Mary Pipher, *Reviving Ophelia: Saving the Selves of Adolescent Girls* (New York: G. P. Putnam's Sons, 1994), p. 202.

8. Laura Shapiro, "Fear and Self-Loathing in Young Girls Lives," *Newsweek*, September 22, 1997, p. 69.

9. Center for Media Education, "10 Key Facts about Children and TV," p. 1.

10. James B. Arndorfer, "Beam Out to Tattoo Young Drinkers," *Advertising Age*, May 12, 1997, p. 88.

11. Philip Van Munching, "Next: Beer on a Stick," *The New York Times*, July 26, 1997, p. 21.

12. Ibid.

13. Chuck Ross and Ira Teinowitz, "Beer Ads Had Wide Underage Reach on MTV," *Advertising Age*, January 6, 1997, pp. 4, 36.

14. Combined News Services, "Logos Urge Smoking," *Newsday*, December 15, 1997, p. A19.

15. Katharine Q. Seelye, "Critics Say N.R.A. Uses Safety Campaign to Lure Children," *The New York Times*, November 19, 1997, p. A24.

Chapter 8. Advertising in Sheep's Clothing

1. Jeff Jensen, "Designers Step into Athletic Footwear," *Advertising Age*, February 3, 1997, p. 10.

2. Allison Samuels and John Leland, "Uh, What's Up, Michael, After Your Movie Debut?" *Newsweek*, November 11, 1996, p. 77.

3. Michael Schudson, *Advertising, The Uneasy Persuasion: Its Dubious Impact on American Society* (New York: BasicBooks, 1984), p. 101.

4. Erik Larson, *The Naked Consumer: How Our Private Lives Become Public Commodities* (New York: Henry Holt, 1992), pp. 187–188.

5. Glen Macnow, "Wearing What Eagles Dare," *The Philadelphia Inquirer*, October 20, 1990, p. 1A.

6. Leslie Savan, *The Sponsored Life: Ads, TV, and American Culture* (Philadelphia: Temple University Press, 1994), p. 2.

7. Eric Clark, *The Want Makers: The World of Advertising* (New York: Viking, 1988), p. 366.

8. Schudson, p. 102.

9. Savan, pp. 1–2.

10. "Reebok Settles Movie Dispute," *The New York Times*, October 6, 1997, p. D2.

11. Joshua Hammer and Corie Brown, "Licensed To Shill," *Newsweek*, December 15, 1997, p. 43.

12. Clark, p. 367.

13. Jean Halliday, "Jackson Lets Ford Star in His Latest Music Video," *Advertising Age*, May 19, 1997, p. 10.

14. Stephen Fox, *The Mirror Makers: A History of American Advertising and Its Creators* (New York: William Morrow, 1984), p. 212.

15. Savan, p. 306.

16. Robyn Meredith, "G.M. Sponsors a Maker of Documentaries and Reaches PBS Viewers 15 Seconds at a Time," *The New York Times*, November 3, 1997, p. D12.

Chapter 9. Brave New World

1. Erik Larson, *The Naked Consumer: How Our Private Lives Become Public Commodities* (New York: Henry Holt, 1992), p. 81.

2. Ibid., p. 63.

3. Ibid., p. 8.

4. Ibid., p. 11.

5. Eric Clark, *The Want Makers: The World of Advertising* (New York: Viking, 1988), p. 166.

6. Ibid., pp. 169–170.

7. Ibid., pp. 175–177, and Claritas company, personal communication with author, 1997.

8. Larson, pp. 48, 222–223.

9. Ibid., pp. 152–154.

10. Ibid., pp. 138–140.

11. Ibid., p. 163.

12. Ibid., p. 55.

13. Ibid., pp. 53–54.

14. Stephen Fox, *The Mirror Makers: A History of American Advertising And Its Creators* (New York: William Morrow, 1984), p. 50.

Glossary

advertising agency—A company that creates and places advertising.

advertorial—A combination of advertising and editorial that is provided by an advertiser.

borrowed interest—Unrelated images or text used to attract attention to an advertisement.

brand—An invented name given to a product to make it stand out from the others.

clickstream—A record of the path (from one Web page to another) taken by an Internet user.

commission—A fee paid to an advertising agency for placing an ad.

cookie—A file placed on a user's computer by a Web site operator that enables the operator to recognize that particular user the next time he or she visits the site.

copywriter—A person who writes the text portion of an ad.

deceptive advertising—Advertising that is intentionally designed to deceive the consumer.

editorial—The content portion of a newspaper or magazine; the articles, stories, or reports, as opposed to the advertising.

focus group—A gathering of people, selected to represent potential buyers of a particular product. Guided by a trained facilitator, they provide input on advertising or marketing programs.

geodemographics—Information about people based on where they live.

infomercial—An advertisement that contains a large amount of information and is therefore longer than a traditional ad.

intermercial—A short commercial on an Internet Web site that can be accessed by clicking a button.

marketing research—A study to provide information useful in the design, marketing, or advertising of a product.

microtargeting—Advertising that is so focused that the advertiser can hand-pick each individual prospect.

motivational research—Studies to determine what influences consumer purchases.

perceived difference—A way to distinguish one product from another in the mind of the consumer, despite whether there is a real difference.

press release—An announcement issued by a company that provides news or information about its business or products.

product positioning—Creating a specific place in the market for a product by promoting it to a particular type of buyer.

service journalism—Designing an editorial framework that will attract advertisers.

spam—Unsolicited e-mail advertisements sent to large numbers of on-line service subscribers at once.

stereotype—A set view of a class of people based on a single characteristic such as their race or religion.

subliminal advertising—A controversial technique that supposedly allows advertising messages to be transmitted to people without their knowledge.

synchographics—Timing advertising messages to key buying points in a consumer's life: birth, graduation, purchase of a home, and so on.

testimonial—An endorsement, usually by a noncelebrity, of a product by someone who has used it.

voice-over—A technique used in television advertising in which an unseen person speaks authoritatively about a product.

Further Reading

Barnards, Neal. *Advertising: Distinguishing Between Fact and Opinion*. San Diego: Greenhaven Press, 1991.

Dunn, John. *Advertising*. San Diego: Lucent Books, 1996.

Frisch, Carlienne. *Advertising*. Vero Beach, Fla.: Rourke Enterprises, 1989.

————. *Hearing the Pitch: Evaluating All Kinds of Advertising*. Baltimore: Rosen, 1994.

Gay, Kathlyn. *Caution—This May Be an Advertisement: A Teen Guide to Advertising*. Danbury, Conn.: Franklin Watts, 1992.

Kuchmey, Paula K. *Mad Ads: Advertising in Today's Marketplace*. London: PPI Publishing, 1995.

Wake, Susan. *Advertising*. Ada, Okla.: Garrett Educational Corp., 1991.

Weiss, Ann E. *The School on Madison Avenue: Advertising & What It Teaches*. New York: NAL Dutton, 1980.

Answers from page 55:

(1) The Consumer Protective Institute had been invented by the advertising agency and had never tested anything. This ad for Revco stores was investigated by the FTC. (2) The vegetables were actually resting on marbles placed in the bottom of the bowl. This Campbell's soup ad was later prohibited. (3) The "sandpaper" was a sheet of Plexiglas to which sand had been applied. This ad for Colgate-Palmolive Rapid Shave Cream was challenged by the FTC. The case eventually reached the Supreme Court for a ruling on deceptive trade practices. (4) The car window had been rolled down so there was no glass at all and the "regular window glass" had been smeared with Vaseline. These ads for Libbey-Owens-Ford were challenged by the FTC and withdrawn after a court ruling.

Internet Addresses

Center for Media Education

<http://tap.epn.org/cme/cme_on.html>

The center publishes reports and information about advertising to children, particularly tobacco and alcohol advertising, and on-line privacy.

Children's Advertising Review Unit

<http://www.bbb.org/advertising/
   childrensMonitor.html>

The Children's Advertising Review Unit (CARU) of the Council of Better Business Bureaus reviews advertising directed at children under the age of twelve in the United States and Canada. CARU asks advertisers to voluntarily comply with its Self-Regulatory Guidelines to stop misleading and inaccurate advertising.

Media Awareness Network

<http://www.screen.com/mnet/eng>

This Canadian organization provides educational information for students and teachers about media literacy and critical consumerism.

NabiscoKids® Privacy and Parents page

<http://www.nabiscokids.com/parents/pa_index.html>

This page outlines Nabisco's policy regarding children's on-line privacy.

Media Literacy and Critical Television Viewing Library

<http://www.pta.org/programs/viewlibr.htm>

The National Parent Teachers Association's listing of educational resources about the new television rating system, on-line safety and privacy, television violence, and critical viewing skills.

Index